acumen
Literary Journal

103

May 2022

Editor: Danielle Hope
4 Thornhill Bridge Wharf,
Caledonian Road, London N1 0RU

Founder and Advisory Editor: Patricia Oxley

Book Reviews Editor: Andrew Geary
25 Southbrook Drive, Cheshunt, Herts. EN8 0QJ
acumenreviews@gmail.com

Interviews Editor: David Perman

All submissions will be carefully considered.
For postal submissions, SAE or IRC is essential for our reply and
return of your typescripts. To submit online, see website:
acumen-poetry.co.uk.
Please send all books for review to the Reviews Editor.

Subscription Rates:

One Year's Subscription
(January, May, September) £15 (UK),
£23 or €35 (Europe), £31 or $55 (USA, rest of world).
pdf version (overseas) £16 or €22 or $26 or equiv.

Single Copies
£5.50 (UK), €10 (Europe), $20 (USA, rest of world).

Advertising rates on request.

Cover designed by Steve Weeks.

ISSN 0964-0304

Visit us on www.acumen-poetry.co.uk

CONTENTS

Editorial

Who would have thought that after the world being consumed for more than two years with a raging pandemic, we would now find a new appalling war exploding? It is as if the first Horseman of the Apocalypse, on his white horse, representing conquest and invoking pestilence, is not enough. Now, we have the second, the creator of war.

As it happened, we had organised reviews of two bi-lingual texts, which now seem to have special significance. Volha Napayeva, a contemporary Belarusian poet, who speaks out against state repression and war, authors one of the books reviewed (see page 90). The other poet, Arkseny Tarkovsky, was born in Yelisavetgrad, Kherson Governorate, formerly the Russian Empire and now Kropyvnytskyi, Ukraine. He was arrested for writing, with friends, an acrostic about Lenin; was wounded in World War II, and was well qualified to write about wars, Stalin's purges and more.

Perhaps the events of the time have coloured my selection for this issue, although it is too early to have received poems about current conflicts. I was particularly pleased to include Rebecca Gethin's poem, "A Refuge", Wendy French's "Truth" and Patrick Osada's "Sunflower", the last of these providing the inspiration for our cover. There are many more excellent poems that resonate with present-day themes and all of life. Thank you to all the writers who submitted work.

You will have observed the return of the *Acumen* interview. If there are poets that you would particularly like to be interviewed, please let me know. In this issue, Caroline Carver talks about the influences of the sea and of language, and how she often writes from "the back of my head", digging "into a space that's special and often secretive".

Thank you again for your continued support of *Acumen*, and your welcome to me as a new, and still learning, editor. I hope you find things to enjoy on these pages. Many of you liked the Goethe quote at the end of my last editorial. We have another new translation of Goethe in this issue. I leave you with Emily Dickinson (whose work is considered anew in this *Acumen*) and wish you peace, with, as she said: "The dearest ones of time, the strongest friends of the soul – books."

Rebecca Gethin

A Refuge

A family who nobody knew moved into the house
with no windows and a hole in the roof.

There was hay to sleep on and they collected sticks
from the forests on the mountain

to light a fire in the middle of the room,
kitchen chairs arranged in a circle of warmth.

They laid the table on the terrace with cutlery and plates
they found in the cupboard and sat down to lunch

on nothing. Not even a *ghiro*. They'd clink the glasses
and shout *Chin Chin* but had no wine.

They banged their spoons and knives on the plates
talked loudly of food they liked. When war broke out

they upped and left the village, so the stones in the walls
were lifted to repair damage in others.

Note: ghiro is the edible dormouse that Italian peasants used to have to eat

Lisa Lopresti

Claymore

Claymore is strength, defence with threats of violence
but things are never as straight forward as that,
for there is a protective hilt with a dual cutting edge
and an explosive percussion that can trip wire you
to the other side in fragments of flesh.
A durable symbol of a deterrent, a negotiation
tool, coercion and distorted images in the blade.
A family name   weaponised.

Wendy French

Truth

The air asks the wind about the silence
it carries
and the wind scours the mountain
for a reply
but the mountain looks down
on the departing river
the river that carries the stone
to the fading sea's edge
the stone does not speak
of the weight that it carries.
Silence likes you to ask it questions
because it knows there is no reply.

The child asks the teacher
What is silence?

When no one speaks the teacher says
but the child does not believe her.

Nicholas Hogg

War Report

In the burnt-out school near Goražde, where the sheaves of sagging plaster
peeled like pages from the wall, or on the road to Asmara, the bombed-out

tanks like wrecks of dark, I'd sought out bullet holes and shrapnel,
the broken buildings. There used to be a factory at the end of my street,

the gate chained shut, but the fence cut through by a boy like me.
Stoning the glass and climbing inside, listening for the glue sniffers

lurking in the basement, the echo of a life that shuttled in the typing pool.
I remember sifting out a desk in a vacant office, and finding

a letter – an everyday chit about pounds and pence, supply
and demand – signed off with a flourish. Holding the ink to the light

like a scholar or a priest, and poised in a shell of ruined brick,
where a lone cloud peered through a hole in the roof,

I'd voiced the blue blood that traced a name: an incantation, a spell,
to bring back the dead.

Féilim James

Song for the Dispossessed

They come to me in the silence of night,
Pulsing through the embroidered sky:
A young girl with blood on her thigh,
Her shoulders bare under starlight.

They come to me when words alight:
A father of four in a Xinjiang prison,
Aching, recalling the smiles of his children,
The sounds of their breathing at night.

They come to me when the moon is in flight:
Five-year-old Riham holding on
To her sister's shirt in the Syrian sun,
One eye on the five-storey height.

They come to me as night unspools:
Images like a smothered scream
Flash, disperse, sharp as a gleam,
Elusive as fish in pools.

And you, my father, embroiled in your sad fight
For dignity, trapped in the talons of her clutch:
When night has held out its cold hand to touch,
You come to me, and my heart turns white.

Kathleen McPhilemy

Binsey

From Bossom's Boatyard to Binsey Lane
the unmade road - stones, baked earth -
whitens under summer sunlight,
darkens in winter, after rain.
The old walls of Frideswide's church
settle into themselves, undisturbed
by intermittent marryings and buryings.

There are so few places where nothing happens
where armed cars don't roll through the streets
where doors aren't burst open at strange hours;
nearly four hundred years since troops of horse
clopped perhaps on this path from their billet
on their way to Oxford to defend the king.

Fifty years ago, in my mother's fields
soldiers rose from the grass, like dragon's teeth,
armed, in camouflage; under their gaze
home was redesignated enemy territory.
Those who come here from eventful places
stare with envy at these easy acres
as they trudge towards the Treacle Well.

Clair Chilvers

For Beirut,
A cento

I
Lebanon shall be turned into a fruitful field

a fountain of gardens,
a well of living waters, and streams from Lebanon,
as beautiful as the famed city of Atlantis.
Walk through the lonely ancient woods
hear the voices from the Cedars of Lebanon.
Purity, love and perfection adorn her every season.
This place is within me; this place is Utopia.

II
Let fire devour the cedars of Lebanon

Small explosions like firecrackers
then the huge blast erupted
blast-waves shuddered through the city
destroying buildings, shattering glass
cutting down people
as they walked in the streets
walking wounded, dozens bleeding
dead pulled from the rubble
a ship anchored off the port on fire
a mushroom cloud into the air
like a nuclear explosion
not a natural catastrophe
this was a massacre.

III
Surely I will make thee a wilderness

Her fiancé led her funeral procession
to the church in which they were to be married
everything you wanted
will be present
except you
in the white wedding dress.
You broke my back my love
you broke my heart.
Life has no taste now that you are gone.
Abraham
Where is your son
He's lying dead
On a street in Lebanon.

Sources: 1.Isaiah 29:17; 2,3. Song of Solomon 4:15; 4,7,8. Ozioma Ogbail: Utopia; 5,6. John K Trainer: Cedars of Lebanon; 9. Judges 9:15; 10-22 & 24-32. Times Newspaper and BBC coverage; 23. Jeremiah 22:6; 33-36. 'r': Lebanon

Adam Day

In Degrees

A window is not
a wall, but both

are empty. It's just
this, as it is. Slow

rain in alders. Hard
to tell if the tree

is holding up
the house or

the house, the tree.

Caroline, one of the central themes in your poetry is the sea. You have sometimes been flippant about it, describing the sea as 'a river grown too big for its boots'. But mainly you respect the sea and regard it as much more important than any of us give it credit for. The title of one of your collections is Fish Eaters: cross any ocean and you touch the matter of the world. *Tell us about your relationship with the sea.*

I can never remember a life without it somewhere near it. I'm told that when I was two and a half, I walked into the sea at Hayling Island, wearing my smart new leggings and shiny shoes. It was Christmas Day. Someone had to run in, fully clothed, to get me back.

I lived for a long time on the Great Lakes in Canada, more than 2,000 miles inland, but was comforted by the sound of ocean-going ships as they made their way through the Seaway. Jamaica was a special paradise, with rainforest and mountains on one side and the transparent blue sea on the other. All my family were and are sailors and I can't count the number of times I've travelled the Atlantic in ships, from banana boats to smart liners. It strikes me that no view is ever complete without a glimpse of water, fresh or salty. These days my husband and I live in in Cornwall, two minutes' walk from the sea.

Your collection, Fish Eaters*, came out of your residency begun in 2013 at the new Marine Institute of Plymouth University.* Fish Eaters *is a large-scale, celebratory book with illustrations by your students and other members of the faculty. But it is also a poetic presentation of ocean science. You said one of the challenges in writing those poems was to reflect on scientific matters without letting a poem become a piece of prose, or without going into too much technical detail. Most reviewers thought you succeeded in the challenge – but why did you undertake the challenge in the first place?*

I was working among scientists, rather pleased with myself for "hot-desking" for the first time. During the entire residency, I was always told I could do exactly as I liked and I felt it important to write about some of the science; but make the poems accessible to a wider audience than just poetry boffins. "Pole of Inaccessibility" is one I'm pleased with as it came together with a mix of fantasy and fact side by side. It's been much anthologised in non-poetry publications, and was recently read by Canadian government scientists in the Arctic, and even Michael Palin. Forgive small puff on that one, but it a great feeling to achieve a goal like that. My muskox poem which is in my new collection has been read by muskox farmers in Alaska.

There's a wonderful photo of you in your residency at Plymouth University, surrounded by faculty members and students – all with broad grins. They obviously enjoyed your residency. Did you enjoy teaching students about poetry and the marine environment? And did you receive much in return from the students?

That photo is actually of students on the publishing course at Plymouth University, the day *Fish Eaters* was launched, but I had met and worked with some of them and without exception they were all great.

My role was never to teach, as such. I ran a small writing group which met at lunchtime once a week and some great stuff came out of that. The Marine Institute building still has my poetry written on its walls and on the stone outside I wrote an article later called "The Building as a Book".

Many of your poems reflect what one reviewer termed your 'unique and individual life experiences'. These included being evacuated in 1940 by convoy to Bermuda, moving to Jamaica, coming back to England for school before emigrating to Canada for 30 years, then working in Europe before settling in Cornwall. One of those life experiences was living in Jamaica and being exposed to the local dialect, or creole. You used that dialect very successfully in 'horse under water', the poem with which you won the National Poetry prize in 1998. Can you tell us what attracted you to Jamaican creole and why you used it?

We lived in Jamaica during the war - the first four years spent on a plantation miles from anywhere. There was a private telephone between four houses; you had to wear rubber-soled shoes to use it or you got an electric shock. There was a telephone exchange, managed by a lovely lady who did a lot of knitting, which seemed to fit in with the cords and plugs she had to manipulate as she connected calls. We had six gramophone records, and listened to ZQI, Jamaica's radio station, but also to Radio Cuba which had a lovely stompy sort of music on it.

And coming round to your question about the dialect, our household was large; several families lived in the old slave quarters and sat singing round an old tree in the evenings. Everyone spoke Jamaican with its irresistible lilt and wonderful words and phrases; it often surprises people to learn that everyone spoke with the accent, white and black alike.

Writing in that dialect could have been controversial. After all, you don't have West Indian ancestry like Benjamin Zephaniah or Linton Kwesi Johnson. Did any of that come out in the reactions to your prize-winning poem?

I did get into a small amount of trouble when *Jigharzi an me* was published, there was correspondence in *Acumen Magazine* about this. Penelope Shuttle came to my rescue arguing that everyone has the right to use other languages. In fact 'horse under water" is on a number of poetry courses, I know of one in Seattle, and David Dabydeen has taught it for many years at Warwick University.

You said: 'I'm not a Jamaican or a Bermudian or a Canadian or even a Cornishwoman but a curious mid-Atlantic mixture of all of these with a bit of Inuit thrown in and therefore somewhat like a coelacanth: confused about origins and the big Why?' That's fascinating – can you expand on it?

Well, we're all a mix aren't we, but I feel my own cultural identity went into overload early on. I was lucky to finish my schooling in Switzerland and Paris, and later was taken by friends on the Grand Tour of Europe, and fell in love with every country we visited, perhaps most especially Italy, which is where our son and family now live. Some days I pick up my heart and ask it, "Where would you like to dream-visit today?" and I'm never sure what it will answer.

You have written many poems about childhood and the point of view of a child. In ju ju baby, *you created a remarkable character – part goblin-child, part infant prodigy – who looks into the present and the past and future and becomes increasingly concerned by what it sees. Tell us where* ju ju baby *came from.*

I've no idea where he came from and of course it's the wrong name, 'ju ju' is an African term, but I confess I just liked the sound of it. And I've been struck how lucky people are who live in remote places and have a great affinity with the world around them. Even in Toronto, I was always aware of living on the ancient Laurentian Shield. So when I wanted to write about Canada, it wasn't the cities but the wilderness that drew me, the joy of paddling a canoe at dusk, of skiing in virtually untouched mountains, the memorable encounters with bears, and I wanted to think about these things through the mind of someone who knew nothing else. And ju ju's advent was blessed by George Szirtes, though he doesn't know it, because he judged the year the ju ju poem about ice-fishing and a jealous ghost was highly commended..

ju ju baby is also a book of adult concern about threats to the natural environment, especially the rapid and steady deterioration of wide-open spaces which support their own distinctive communities and culture. You have travelled extensively in the wilder parts of North Americas, like the Yukon and other Inuit lands in Canada. You know those lands from experience and in your imagination, and you are clearly alarmed at the way they are changing.

I made 'Fresh Air', an hour-long radio documentary about the environment, back in the 1970's. It focussed on a North American Indian who talked about care of the environment and how the Indian people used to recycle things and tend their lands carefully. This cemented my interest in being part of nature, as well as making me aware of environmental problems - quite early, by chance.

It may seem strange that we have come so far into this interview before exploring your great passion for Cornwall. You have lived there for many years, integrating yourself into the culture of the county, organising poetry readings and a festival. And when you became a member of the Falmouth Poetry Group you were quoted as saying that you had come home. Tell us more about you and Cornwall.

Cornwall is such a strange and beautiful landscape: home to eccentrics such as the poet, the Reverend Hawker, who pretended to be a mermaid sometimes, smoked his opium pipe looking out at the sea, fed his sermons to the pigs and was a friend of Tennyson, who said some of Hawker's best work was better than his own. Hawker had two wives, the first 40 years older than himself, the second, 40 years younger. But yes, Cornwall has also been a bit left out of things: we have more saints than anywhere else, I believe, because we were too far away for people to bother striking them off the list. Our sea and beaches and the romantic Scilly Isles work deep into our hearts. The county has contributed importantly to science. My husband is currently involved with uncovering the legacy of a navigation instrument which has recently revisited old haunts by travelling round the world taking measurements. It made an incredible aid to shipping, thereby saving thousands of otherwise shipwrecked lives. It's all go here. And the terrain offers much to the imagination, both good and bad: they say a lot of life's dropouts end up here because they can't get any further away from it all. On the other hand, we have a bumper crop of poets, artists and other craftspeople. The Falmouth Poetry Group, founded by Peter Redgrove and Penelope Shuttle, will be celebrating its 50th year of life in October, and it continues to inspire, attract and produce wonderful writing. I probably wouldn't be enjoying the pleasure of this interview with you, David, if it weren't for them, and of course the National prize. And none of us can forget the light, thanks to the granite we live on, the inherent toughness of its people and their joyful language, and, dare I say it, the old stone circles, the lingering magic one finds everywhere.

You have a new collection, your seventh book, being published this year by Oversteps Books. Can you say something about it?

Ah yes, I am VERY thrilled to have a new book coming, *Cannonball with Feathers*, and big thanks to Alwyn Marriage of Oversteps Books for taking me on again. I won't be as energetic at events, and my bad eyes make reading a bit of a chore at times, though one learns to compensate. The eighties are a time of mystery, not many people write about all the problems and often indignities that come with it, there's no romance in owning up to something like boils, and people treat you as 'past it'. I once was guilty of this myself, I never thought of anyone old as being other than someone to dismiss. Now I'm here I get such a buzz! True, my feet sometimes limp along behind the thought-self which is scurrying through the trees and out to the next view of the sea.

Cannonball is somewhat autobiographical, and tries to blend facts and poetry in a poetic way. I'm thrilled to join the growing band of poets who have produced books in their mid-eighties. I know this will be my last collection because I won't have the stamina to do another. Until a week or so ago, I hadn't looked further ahead. But when I took an

Italian picture to be photo-shopped last week, I found myself thinking 'this will be a wonderful cover for a pamphlet'. I already have the first poem for it, and my notebooks are full of drafts that look as if they'd like to travel. Suddenly it seems I have two books coming out this year, as my work with students at the University of Bucharest is resulting in a bilingual collection.

Caroline, can you tell us something about the way you write? Are you a great reviser or do you write the final version early on?

I write from the back of my head, dig into a space that's special and often secretive. When I write from it I start with one line of thought, and then just put down words as they come, ideas I didn't know were there. These days, if I go to a workshop, I write my name at the bottom of each page. Otherwise, when I return to them later, they have come from such a distant place, I'm not sure whether they're mine, or a draft by someone else, so great is the leap from the back to the front of the head and the kind of trance that comes with it.

In these interviews for Acumen *we often ask the much published interviewees if they have any advice for newer poets about getting published. Is there any advice you would like to pass on?*

We're lucky that there are so many small new presses around now, who are often open to taking a flier on someone new. Some run competitions for new work. But I would say the old tried and true way in is begin with sending work to magazines, they are the best open doorway. (Apologies to Danielle for saying this, I know how swamped editors can become!)

Lastly, there is no longer any shame in producing a self-published pamphlet. They have achieved respectability at last.

And perhaps most of all, everyone should read as keep reading as much poetry as they can find time for.

The interview took place in February 2022
David Perman / Caroline Carver

Roger Harvey

Rooks

Greedy rogues and undertakers, graveyard birds and thieves;
thus maligned along with other crows,
and all unfairly,
to me these rooks are wise in myth and fact,
riding the tall-tree sky beyond my window,
waking up the spring with their clamorous building.

In windy blue or misty distance,
both rude and shy, stern and friendly,
bred for an ancient England and still timeless,
they mark our seasons with an earthy song:
ground bass for sweeter flutings,
counterpoint to changing centuries.

Born into bare twigs,
they rise and fall above lush green tree-tops,
gilded with high sunshine, gleaming like autumn fruit;
transcendent, divine brightness in their eyes and strong with life,
they will caw us into winter too,
through another spring and into summers richer still than this,
perhaps with golden light more pure upon the black,
and music more glorious than any we have heard.

James Appleby

Pillar of Shame

When they take it down, it will be face by face.
I know how they work. To remove it entirely
is not their style, instead they tug at arms,
spooning a socket clean out – slowly,
moving in toes and fingers. Universities,
under strain, can be where we forget,
and though the colour, plastic-orange,
orange of blood in mud, orange that skin might be,
was made to mimic shame, all that will fade.
They'll do something with the space. I know how they work.
A café franchise, padded chairs arranged
to sit online face-first, screen-stuck and -starved,
no plans to meet, a QR on the wall
logging where you are. The pillar?
Dragged to storage, maybe.
First a livid column of flame, then soot in air –
or in the city's soft tissue, needle-first,
but forgotten here.

Jim C Wilson

Elie Wiesel's 'Night'

I read
and read again
of Europe's darkest time
although the plot forever stays
the same.

Sue Kauth

Ready

Moonlight spills like milk on to the flat lake.
At last the guns are silent but a temporary stillness
brings no calm.

Our belongings, those we can carry, those
we have salvaged from the rubble,
lie in a pile beside the doorway
in readiness.

We sit in darkness, keeping watch, listening,
waiting for the man who may, we are praying
take us to safety.

The surface of the lake ripples
as a breeze ruffles the air and briefly
moonlight fragments into spears.

The baby whimpers and cries
but I have no milk for her.
We hear a distant engine and tense
as the sound draws nearer.

We are ready, as ready as we can be, when
moonlight spills like milk on to the lake again,
and the man arrives to carry us to salvation.
Or to something else.

Joan McGavin

The Look

I'm thinking of the look a woman gave
as the mudslide rushed towards her
and she turned her face
upwards and threw
her baby
clear.

I'm thinking what the last person
who saw her saw in her face.

No photo fixes it.
No artist had time
to paint that look.

Rescuers would comment
not on the look –
gone down
under the rearranged earth.
They spoke of a gesture:
all they could say was
she 'seemed like she was
lifting something'.

Mike Barlow

Blue Moon

Once, after the tail-end of a hurricane
had blown through the day – the roaring
in the trees like a passing train and the rain
berserk as it over-ran the valley – once
there was this quiet October evening,

two full moons in one month, two lives
wrought into one lifetime, the perfect
silver globe up there, a symbol of itself,
not blue, in fact, but hung in a deep
indigo sky and stained by its idiom,

the rare and common moment held
like a pause between breaths in which
we might appreciate, as if it were our own,
the life of another, and a friend's passing settles
like a fierce wind suddenly quelled.

Marie Little

Dusk

Six o'clock draws its curtains
twists the dial on chemicals keeping me
sunny. The mood over the field is indigo
blue, heavy with sooty clouds in waiting. I
have no need of litmus paper. I know my score.
Bottles in rows wink at me, each emptied to a
different level, each a slightly different chime in

the tune of dusk. I shun them all, flick
the kettle on. Slide something herby, caffeine-free
from a purple box, steep it so long it might
understand. Drink it in sips, watch the soot spread.
Later the bottles will sing.

Jan FitzGerald

The Warning

A hi-vis hangs from a billboard across the road,
flashing in the wind like a warning
against an invisible enemy.
No one's claimed it
though it's been there for days.

I retreat to the back of the house to make bread.
Maybe some kid will yank the vest down
while I'm watching yeast bubbles rise
and lumps of butter skid around the bottom of the pan
like tiny dodgem cars.

If I roll silky dough around the breadboard
and knead it with vigour,
dusting myself off before easing it into the oven,
maybe I'll think of that painting by Jean-François Millet
of a woman in a head scarf guiding dough
into a bricked hole in the wall –
and I'll be thinking long enough
in a way that's actually not thinking,
to forget the hi-vis billowing in the wind
as if a man had slipped clean out of it

and how people are disappearing
everywhere.

Gill McEvoy

Ivy Wreaths are Multiplying by the River in the Woods

This is a lonely path, and that's what I prefer:
a chance to watch the dipper in the stream,
the deer come down to drink,
the wren that bobs along the bank.
But lately all my pleasure's spoiled by ivy wreaths
hung mysteriously along the way.

Whoever made them did so with great skill,
twining the supple lengths together
three strands at a time, tying them off
with a clever twist of stem. Some of them still fresh,
and some so small they'd fit a child's wrist,
each one a perfect circle.

I ask about them in the village
but no-one seems to know: they say
they have not noticed them, or never
walk that way. And yet I sense evasion
in their words, even those who cry
"Oh, secret art, how wonderful!"

Someone knows, I'm sure, in this, a county
of peculiar beliefs, where even walls
are carved with marks to ward off witchcraft
and the evil eye. They know, but will not say.
I reach a hand to lift one down, then stop,
my mind is screaming 'No, Don't touch! Don't touch –
you don't know what you might be bringing home!'

I tell myself they must be blessings on the trees,
a pleasant fiction and I half believe, until I find
all night they loom and terrorise my sleep.

Patrick Osada

Sunflower

Down at the pub, the rumours had soon spread :
our local farmer's selling off his land.
When goat-man left and pheasant farm shut down,
we realised there was truth in what was said.

Soon, other tenants left their grazing land –
moved horses on, their meadows left to weeds,
rusty with ragwort, pastures overgrown –
a change the roaming deer can't understand.

Birds leave the hedgerows, rabbits on the run
as men and their machines rip up the land;
at the site entrance they erect a sign :
Building Communities For Everyone…

But not for hawthorn, fox, orchid or deer –
those residents have gone, their fields stripped bare.
On this sterile plane earth's heaped in piles,
nothing's left alive on the levels here.

Pipes and bricks arrive all summer long
but, while the men were busy on the site,
nature crept back to green those heaps of soil
and, on the highest, planted something strong.

Unnoticed, this plant grew more each day
till giant golden face turned to the sun.
This was nature's turn, a defiant sign –
two fingers to those stealing land away.

Tim Relf

Long Lines

Bollocks to Laurie Lee – we didn't need some old dude to tell us
how it felt to hide in hedgerows, pockets alive and heavy. Gone,

we were, in folded fields by moon-backed streams, diving
for cover at a dog's bark or a door opening. Poaching, my arse

nobody owns fish, everyone knows that –
so nightly we'd string out lines then return to collect

the spoils: flesh-speckled gifts from another world. But first,
JPS-dizzy and smashed on Spar cider, we'd dance

in carparks and churchyards – singing along
to cassettes. And now, ironing a shirt, about to drive to you,

the word 'cassette' seems as incongruous as 'poaching' did then,
as unreal as 'crematorium' did this morning when I'd googled directions,

as antiquated, I suppose, as the term 'google' itself may one day
come to be. Tomorrow, early, I'll set off –

I'll tread respectful, measured steps,
read careful, well-judged words,

but I'll be stealing along hoof-pocked paths,
doubled-up and clumsy quiet in an August when the Slad Valley was ours –

two wild, uncatchable boys, magicking brown trout
from the racing heart of the world and afterwards, afterwards, dancing.

.Nancy Mattson

Today's Word is Seed

Today's word is seed
Mine was given to save for a month
until dry, then add to a sauce in secret
Swallowed whole, it grew me taller
without swelling my breasts or belly
It was not that kind of seed

I sowed the word in a gap between
root vegetables and peas in labelled rows
Anonymous, it thrived on months of inattention
grew into a knee-high bush with green needles
and baby-fist flowers that popped
into fat berries I'd never seen before

I pruned the bush in autumn
clipped off every Y, harvested a bowl of seeds
pierced, threaded and sewed them
    on the hem of a nightdress to give me dreams
    on the collar of a day dress to make me shine
    on the bodice of an evening dress to help me dance
    on the yoke of a mourning dress to give me tears

Tim Relf

The Poem We've All Written

Michael Henry

Incognito from London

And still they came,
squelching in from a cold Saturday night,
slipping off overshoes, overcoats,
the thawing of their faces mirrored
in the large parquet floor.

And still they came
into the warm sauna of expectation,
the ladder-backed chairs pushed back,
only a tall straight one remaining
for the guest from London to sit on.

And how they bustled about,
Eunice with platters of finger-foods,
her German-Canadian husband
who was a carpet-fitter in Edmonton
setting up the scaffolding for the event.

I expected them to say 'Comrade':
the Rudolf Steiner roadie, a new age
electrician from Devon, and his wife
who wore a long eurythmic skirt,
shocking pink like a loud sneeze.

Then the hero of the evening,
incognito in nondescript suit and tie,
distributing books and pamphlets about
anthropomorphism and the Waldorf School
that only made me think of salad.

David Ball

Between the Trees

Dark even at midday, leaves
stirring in the stillness of the air,
two nymphs emerge, in white,
long classical folds, a silver pin
at one shoulder. Their eyes, dark and shy,
avoid mine, which, dazzled and half-closed,
follow them.

They're laughing, that's right, they're
giggling through this romantic wood.
It's romantic now, is it, this wood,
which I thought was one of Virgil's?
They're laughing at me, I tell you,
the shepherd who, in the spring,
plays his flute. But they too are a part
of the comedy, of the dance:
boy girl, stick flower.

In crowded cities, everyone is in some way
alone, even the couples: they greet no one.
Charles Baudelaire, all by himself, passes me by.
A woman, at two paces, passes him by.
She's the serpent, the pool, the eye of the storm.

Through the fog, which turns
the trees of the square into the ghosts
of hanged men, a woman in black,
her skin pale, her hair heavy and glistening,
a symbolist painting,
an impressionist painting,
wanders, is condemned to wander,
and to take me with her.

Helen Ashley

Catalyst

Don't leave until you have shared with me
this pear: *Doyenne du Comice*,
a most revered fruit.

See its size, greater
than other varieties and rounder,
almost so as to deny its shape
as pyriform.

How easily the blade cuts
through its buttery flesh, and frees
the rich sweet juice,
the delicate perfume.

There, I've placed the bowl between us:
take a slice,
and I shall take one,

and what we thought we had to do,
so urgently,
loses significance, while words
that might have been left unsaid

now hold us,
as tender and sweet
as this fruit you share with me.

Gill Learner

Let it Be Like This

The smell will arrive first – ylang ylang, perhaps,
or sandalwood. It will be followed by a cloud
of a colour never seen before: this will surround me,
block the light. Faintly at first I'll hear music – violins
and cellos at the start, then, as the volume grows,
the rumble of a double bass. Soon woodwind
will join in and maybe, just audible above the rest,
a theramin will add its eerie voice.
                                        I will stand
for several minutes, breathing in the scents, then
lie down on a surface, warm and spongy soft,
which will cradle my tired bones. I will stretch out
in Savasana as the music swells and fades.
Slowly my flesh will soften, dissolve and rise
to become one with the cloud.

Gavin Lyon

Care-taker

I think that one day,
on a whim,
you will set me a task
I cannot achieve -
perhaps to sweep
all the sand from a beach
into the ever-turning tide.
On the off chance
I will buy a broom
and await the possibility.

Matthew Smith

House of Many Things

Under the mat outside
a key is shining.

The hall is silent,
motes a little unsettled.
An old 10p coin in a
cedar drawer. Dimples
in the carpet where a bed
was footed. Small blackboard
for notices scrubbed clean.

You listen to the wind
in the warp of a casement.

A memory comes:
holding on to the handle
of a window blown in a storm,
impossible to close,
metal burning skin.
Much shouting
and the wind beyond
booming with the holler
of a djinn.

A scuffle downstairs
behind a closed door.

Mum's room.

Dead flies fall
from the red blind that closes
on the sun like a swollen eyelid.

Many things are lost
as you pass. The walls
shed their maps,
whitewashed.

Finally, the back door
and the back yard.
Night's backdrop
of dull stars.

The key, hidden again.
The only thing that shines here.

Steam rises
from a mug of coffee
by the woodblock,
hurried by the wind.

Elizabeth Rapp

Knockout Spring

Suddenly the world is full of it,
pushy, look at me spring,
turning handstands on the grass.

She explodes in a shower of gold
crams the sun in her mouth
as if she's starving.

Squaring up to winter,
she punches him on his icicled nose
knocks him out cold.

INNER THAN THE BONE: Another look at the poems of EMILY DICKINSON

Duncan Forbes

From the first posthumous edition of her work in 1890 till now, Emily Dickinson's reputation has grown prodigiously. Her complete surviving manuscript poems have been transcribed and printed in putative order of composition, a variorum edition has been published and she has been the subject of numerous selections, commentaries and biographies. Harvard and Amherst have websites devoted to her work, rooms in museums there contain relics of her life and her poems seem to have travelled far and wide in the English-speaking world and beyond. Her 'story' or 'legend' is thought to be well known but, as Lyndall Gordon says in her 2010 biography, 'Emily Dickinson is now recognised as one of the greatest poets who ever lived, yet her life has remained a mystery.'

Generations of readers have been increasingly drawn to her utterly distinctive poems and the astonishing voltage of her lines: 'My life closed twice before its close – ', 'I heard a Fly buzz – when I died –', 'Ourself behind ourself concealed', 'It might be lonelier/ Without the Loneliness – ' ....

Emily Dickinson takes the conventional themes of lyric poetry (nature, love, time, religion, death) and gives them fresh and quizzical force, often in hymn-like iambic quatrains that are in style and content utterly unlike any hymn ever written or sung. The poems use the first person singular to interrogate and dramatise whatever the writer elects to encounter or 'italicise'. There are graphic, inquisitive and often ecstatic encounters with the natural world, such as a jay in winter, a maybug in summer, a red flower or a sudden thunderstorm. A meeting with a snake ('A narrow fellow in the grass') provides an almost sexual frisson and induces 'zero at the bone'. Indeed, if we were to judge a poet simply by 'frisson per line', her work would score highly.

As a poet Dickinson is able to anatomise depression and bleak despondency with a consolatory finesse 'inner than the bone'. As she said in a letter, 'Abyss has no biographer' and yet, like Hopkins, she was an expert explorer of sudden depths ('Such sumptuous – Despair') and vast profundities ('finite infinity'). Like a dramatist, she can soliloquise about disturbance and even derangement in a few well chosen words.

'I felt a Funeral, in my Brain,' is a poem to be read entire for its images evoking numbness and nullity. And then there is the poem 'The first Day's Night had come – '(J 410) about some sort of debilitating nervous breakdown. The following quotation begins at stanza three of five:

> And then – a Day as huge
> As Yesterdays in pairs,
> Unrolled its horror in my face –
> Until it blocked my eyes –
>
> My Brain – began to laugh –
> I mumbled – like a fool –
> And tho' 'tis Years ago – that Day –
> My Brain keeps giggling – still.
>
> And Something's odd – within –
> That person that I was –
> And this One – do not feel the same –
> Could it be Madness – this?

'The Brain – is wider than the Sky'. No wonder she asked of Shakespeare, 'Why is any other book needed?' As Robert Frost once remarked of Emily Dickinson, poets need not go to Niagara to write about the force of falling water.

> I never saw a Moor –
> I never saw the Sea –
> Yet know I how the Heather looks
> And what a Billow be.

Over 140 of her nearly 1800 surviving poems begin with that word 'I'. With all those first person pronouns in her poems centring upon self, it is tempting and indeed inviting to read the works as primarily autobiographical but they can also be imaginative performances, brisk dramatic monologues whose confessional intensity leads us rapidly into an inner arena of her and our own making. In a letter dated July 1862, Emily Dickinson sought to distance herself from her creations: 'When I state myself, as the Representative of the Verse – it does not mean – me – but a supposed person.' She also acknowledges the potent force of language to affect readers over the years:

> A Word dropped careless on a Page
> May stimulate an eye
> When folded in perpetual seam
> The Wrinkled Maker lie
>
> Infection in the sentence breeds
> We may inhale Despair
> At distances of Centuries
> From the Malaria –

As a writer, she was much preoccupied with death and what might lie beyond and with what she called the soul. In the meticulous edition of the Complete Poems edited by Thomas H. Johnson and first published in 1955, there is a compendious Subject Index and 'Death' takes up more than a column, whereas 'Soul' accounts for half a column's worth of references. In addition to 'the culprit – Life', 'the quiet nonchalance of Death' may be a preoccupation of hers, but she sees it in many different ways and lights. Her poems imagine losing consciousness, dying itself, being buried, adjustment in the tomb, being welcomed by a fellow corpse, death as sleep or endless rest, as a gateway to eternity, as decomposition, as a temporary state, as extinction or an infinity of nothing:

> Until the moss had reached our lips
> And covered up our names.

Her famous and disorientating lyric beginning 'Because I could not stop for Death' is a symbolic encounter with mortality and eternity in the setting of a small town in a huge universe. Life ('labor and ... leisure') is characterised as a long day's journey to the graveyard, where immortality beckons and yet the horses' heads are 'toward eternity'. Intensely physical and metaphysical, this dream-like dramatic lyric on the theme of Death and the Maiden has become one of her most celebrated and disturbing reflections on time, death, life on earth and eternity.

Earnest though her poems may often seem, there is also penetrating wit and lightness of touch which turns her sceptical satire into amusement: 'I'm Nobody! Who are You?' Her doubts about conventional religion and its certainties can be expressed in a trenchant metaphor or two:

Those – dying then,
Knew where they went –
They went to God's Right Hand –
That Hand is amputated now
And God cannot be found –

The abdication of Belief
Makes the Behaviour small –
Better an ignis fatuus
Than no illume at all –

For her, it's as if dogma and doctrine in all their aspects are open to question: 'I don't like Paradise –// Because it's Sunday – all the time – /And recess never comes – '.

In the same irreverent poem (J 413), God's alleged omniscience, for instance, is dismissed with sceptical doubt in a terse image depicting God as an eternal spyglass if not spy: 'but they say/Himself – a Telescope/Perennial beholds us –'.

Time and again, her first-person poems invite us to re-examine ourselves and our beliefs in the light of freshly expressed and often cryptic enquiries. Indeed, as Lyndall Gordon argues: 'I want to propose that her poems work when a theorem is applied to a *reader's* life. It's a mistake to spot Dickinson in all her poems; the real challenge is to find ourselves.'

In her biography, *Lives Like Loaded Guns: Emily Dickinson and her Family's Feuds*, Gordon examines her own conjecture that Dickinson suffered from epilepsy, like her Dickinson nephew, Ned, and her cousin Zebina Montague. Lyndall Gordon adduces much relevant evidence from Dickinson's life and work. On the evidence presented, I think epilepsy more than possible, indeed plausible, and yet probably unproveable, as a lawyer might say. It might help to explain her solitary choices and her many intense poems of breakdown but equally these may have been determined by psychological rather than physiological causes.

The story of specifically American poetry in English is sometimes taken to begin with two contrasting and strikingly American Nineteenth Century 'Pioneers': Whitman ('I Sing the Body Electric') and Dickinson ('The Soul selects her own Society'). Although they can both be described as visionary writers, they represent very different but distinctive types of American poetry and poetic personalities. Walt Whitman, embracing, rapturous, wordy and affirmative, enjoys a sense of redemptive empathy with the natural world and common humanity. Emily Dickinson, on the other hand, is less often ecstatic than terse, solitary, questioning and troubled, as she puzzles over life's enduring mysteries: love, life and death, what they mean and what (if anything) lies beyond them. Walt Whitman threw himself into self-publication and self-promotion, whereas Emily Dickinson withdrew into prolific poetic obscurity and increasing solitude, despite bold entreaties from Helen Hunt Jackson that she should publish her work. ('You are a great poet – and it is wrong to the day you live in, that you will not sing aloud. When you are what men call dead, you will be sorry you were so stingy.' Letter, March 20, 1876)

What then are her weaknesses as a poet? Principally, and only on occasion in my view, repetition, flimsiness, feyness and whimsicality. Because she preserved so much, she preserved the unevenness and failures which a more fastidious published poet might be at pains to suppress. She can sometimes sound trite and twee, or quaint, mawkish and inconsequential but not often and not for long. Not all her poems sustain the quality of their best lines but that would be difficult. It is possible to be arrested by a line, often the startling opening line, and then be disappointed by the last lines or so of the same short verse or verses.

Fewer than twenty of Emily Dickinson's poems were published during her lifetime (the number gradually increases as modern scholarship discovers more) and those texts were tidied and emended by her conventionally minded editors. The distinctive punctuation or lack of it in favour of the dash gives the manuscript poems their highly idiosyncratic appearance on the printed page, though in his selection of 1959 the poet and editor James Reeves regularized the punctuation 'as surely she would have expected had her poems been published in her lifetime' (Thomas H. Johnson). I wonder. With their breathy dashes, quirky capitals and breezily disconcerting slant rhymes, the poems seem like encoded cryptograms with their own notations for the inner voice to articulate by receiving their open-ended images, impulsive rushes and dubious hesitancies on the mind's ears and freshly opened eyes. Once one accepts the original formats in which we have discovered the poems, it is hard to see them otherwise.

Great Streets of silence led away
To Neighbourhoods of Pause –
Here was no Notice – no Dissent
No Universe – no Laws –

By Clocks, 'twas Morning, and for Night
The Bells at Distance called –
But Epoch had no basis here
For period exhaled.

Why did someone so very acute as Dickinson and so inwardly sure of her literary merit if not 'neglected genius' rely on frail hidden manuscripts and capricious posterity to publish and publicise her work? Or did she no longer care? 'This is my letter to the World'. But it could so easily not have been and the secret poems might have been destroyed, perhaps burnt, along with all the correspondence to her. For, at her request, her sister Lavinia destroyed the letters to Dickinson. As far as I know, she left no specific wishes to her unofficial literary executor, except to leave Vinnie 'everything'. The poet's unworldliness towards her own literary remains has led to many problems and to the preservation of scraps and fragments which, however interesting to the scholar of minutiae, can distract or even detract from her astonishing achievement. There's an odd mixture here of defiant perfectionism and casually prolific improvidence. It's as if the posthumous caches of almost 1800 poems said or say take us or leave us but on our own terms.

This World is not Conclusion
A Species stands beyond –
Invisible, as Music –
But positive, as Sound –

For further reading and of great interest:

Dickinson: Selected Poems and Commentaries by Helen Vendler (Harvard 2010)
Lives Like Loaded Guns: Emily Dickinson and her Family's Feuds by Lyndall Gordon (Virago Press 2010)

Rebecca Gethin

Sei Solo

Lifting the violin of his heart
from his body, he balances it between
chin and clavicle and an outstretched arm.

He strokes arteries and veins
with their pipework and gristles.
Fingertips know the exact touch.

The breath of the sounding core
voices a music that might shatter
its body of thin flame. As he plays on

a ghost sings out from the depths
as her voice rises into existence,
drawing her into the air we believe in.

He holds steady and whole. At the close,
the heartwood falls still and she's here till
the door clicks behind her as the last note fades.

Sei solo (translates as: you are alone) is a note Bach wrote on the manuscript of his Partita No 9 which is said to refer to the sudden death of his beloved first wife, Maria Barbara.

Philip Rush

William Henry Edward Rush
(1897-1946)

The story goes, he said he never thought
    he'd live to see the rationing of bread
and he never did. The certificate
    describes in detail the circumstances:

an electric train at Willesden Junction,
   different, quiet and dark. Official
accident records say nothing at all.
   There were whispers, of course there were.
But all the years I knew her,
   my grandmother spoke hardly a word.

Elizabeth Barton

Absence

In the quiet forest, nothing stirs.
I hear no sigh of leaves, no woodlark's song,
only the moaning of the bracken.

I see your boot prints in the sand, puddled
with rain, the claws of a dog beside you.
Your lips are silent as the pines encircling us.

I follow you across the heath, past bones
of birch, faded moor-grass, heather.
You teach me not to fear the adder's hiss,

point to vanished things –
ancient barrows, herds of aurochs, tarpan.
You show me how a kestrel's wings

blossom in the emptiness of sky and heath,
how the gorse flower burns with a wild light.
I feel the chill of rain on eyes, ears, lips

and in the gloom, I see the ruby glow
of toadstools, moss the green of paradise.
Far off, I hear you whistling for your dog.

D.W. Evans

The Other One

Opening the blue door of a shed he had called
The Other One,
his old straw hat tips from a nail,
doffed by a breeze predicting a storm.

Its crown's unwinding like a work unfinished,
black band sweat salted -
so much garden slog
under a few retirement years of sun.

So little left to show for it, all that slog.
A year untended, and where are the flowers
of yesteryear? Slug shit mostly,
piled up against trunks of weeds.

A god dies and its universe goes to pot.
I'll keep his trowels and other diggy,
clawing stuff, though containers and planters
begin and end my Eden.

His hat I'll let the wind take -
deliver it to the other dimension,
presumably somewhere up north?

Caroline Johnstone

The Problem with Dust

Grief is weary in the waiting
and gathering of itself and the dust to dust
for a solemn parade of flat-footed undertakers.

You can try to clean it away,
try to hide from it like a hermit
but it will curl itself under doors
creep past closed curtains
seep through any crevice
as if it needed to announce
its presence over and over again
so you pour it on to your
corn flakes,
stir into your tea like ashes.

John Saunders

Ghosts

They are on all the platforms
trapped in a world parallel
to the temporal,
as if the old theology
of Guardian Angels by our side,
has come to pass;
belief transubstantiated
into secular delusion.

Their profiles remain,
in the present tense,
there is an absence of recent messages,
and each year we are prompted
to wish them a happy birthday,
their best photo smiling at us.

Jeremy Page

His Last Swim

Wilfred Owen at Folkestone, August 1918

It's more than a century since
the poet left his hotel
to spend that blissful afternoon
a safe distance from
the edge of England
with no thought beyond
his movements through
the *fast bright* waves
no sense of any endings.

Grateful for the *serenity*
the insistent calm of those moments
and for his undiluted joy
and the *supreme sun* that would set
soon but not soon enough for him
on that war to end all wars
and his own drawing down of blinds.

Virginia Betts

Two Benches

I never imagined this.
Outside a blank, white room,
with its blank, white walls.
Inside, the clock unwinds;
seconds drip steadily down the line,
waiting for nature to call time.

On a cold metallic bench
I wait, suspended;
Stop-motion faces speed by;
nothing changes,
but nothing is the same.

Streaming in, glassy light is prismed through the pane;
the sky bright and empty;
seagulls scream silently;
white ornamental frieze, framed against the blue.

And later, on a broken bench in the bay,
I watch the white-topped waves constantly returning home;
still in the blank, white room;
still seeing your blank, wide stare.

Ciaran McDermott

Megaceros Hibernicus

After Barrie Cooke

An echo rebounded through thicketed oak
and washed loose in the weeping
bellies of streams,
smudged reproduction of an original
reduced to rumour,
cave wall protest against the vanishing-
mere shadow of an outline clutched
and fumbled by the mind, each fresh purchase
a little weaker, relinquishing more
of the incomprehensible length of horned bone,
the seismic flank, the pelt-heat shriek
of immanence-pricked spear-tip
of a million-year-thrust of kings towards the hissing rut

hooves stampeding soundless across oceans.

Patricia Helen Wooldridge

Dear Darkness

When I can't sleep…

I get up, make camomile tea, slice an apple, sit in bed, read or write in my journal about night-waking

I seize the chance to witness what I'm thinking or blank it out with sudoku, for worry-time has no sleep

when fear creeps inside my head and death slips in the doorway – how many die in their sleep?…

now I have to rise, feed the cat, move to another room, light a candle, who else is up at this hour?

or I go into the garden wishing I could see more, to touch both you and your stars

what it must be like to see a path through trees where night memory is my vision

it takes twenty minutes for pupils to dilate and even then on a night with no moon

I can't tune in to your shadows – everything reduced to black and grey and my ears become alert

it's only 3.00 am but at least I've caught the slip-stitch of time…

night sky holding
a bowl of infinity
over our heads

Matt Bryden

Rich and Poor in the Underworld

I should choose, so I might live on Earth, to serve as the hireling of another, some landless man with hardly enough to live on, rather than be lord over all the dead that have perished.
Odyssey 11, 489 – 491

See this tanned thick-hammed youth
and his paramour emerge short-sleeved
onto a seagull-padded platform.

Treading lightly, they seem already stripped,
refined by flame to their present forms.
Yet neither has suffered the lightning flash

or ritual to take them below. To be weightless,
inconsequent requires you crack your bones, slip blood
from its vein, a report like a shot jolt

spirit from skin. Beneath them, cobblers and sweeps –
shorn of the slights and shocks that rocked
their eyelids closed – turn wide circles, swirl about

as weightless, inconsequent as cry-baby Achilles.
His demands for attention register
as disharmony, a rift. While our more imperial man

attempts to kick up the dust, raise a 5 iron
against a backdrop forest fire, cut a swathe
like a motorcade through traffic.

How we tire. Press fingers to our lips
and turn our gaze; as Ajax rattles arms
in the tomb, shoos the draughts players away.

Charles Baudelaire (1821-1867)

Baudelaire was a French poet, essayist and art critic. This poem, *Le Flacon*, sometimes translated as *The Perfume Flask,* was censored from the 1857 edition of his famous work, *Les Fleurs du Mal.*

The Perfume Bottle

Some perfumes are so strong they suffuse
the most solid substance. It's as if they soak
through glass. There are times when you unlock
a casket brought back from the East, wards and keys

grinding in protest, or a cupboard, rife
with black dust and the past's bitter smell,
in an empty house – and you find a small bottle
from which a departed soul springs back to life.

A crowd of thoughts lay dormant, deathly pupae
gently trembling in dark shadows.
Now they unfurl their wings, lifting their bodies
spangled with gold, glossed with pink, tinged blue.

Memory rises, dazing the mind, flutters
in murky air; eyes close as giddiness
takes hold, dragging its victim by force
towards an abyss darkened by corpses' gas.

He lies, overwhelmed, on the brink of an ancient pit
where an old love's ghostly remains, decayed,
stir awake, like Lazarus tearing his shroud,
stinking of the tomb, yet still touching the heart.

When no one remembers who I am, when I'm
merely an old bottle, worn out, abject,
thrown in the back of some foul cupboard – cracked,
abandoned, thick with grease, dust and grime,

I'll be your coffin, my kindly plague, as proof
of your virulent power – sweet poison prepared
by angels, liquor consuming me like an acid
and bringing death to my heart with the gift of life.

Translated from the French by **Antony Mair**

Heinrich Lersch (1889-1936)

Lersch was a German World War I soldier and worker poet.

Brothers

Before our tangled wire there lay a corpse in plainest view,
Warmed daily by the sunshine and cooled by wind and dew.

I looked into his face, as he lay there every day,
And ever more the feeling grew that there my brother lay.

Every hour I saw him, lying on the ground,
And heard his voice from peaceful times ring out with joyful sound.

Often was I woken by a cry which grieved me sore:
"My brother, dearest brother, do you love me no more?"

Until, despite the bullets, I went when day had flown,
And brought him back – and buried him – a comrade quite unknown.

My eyes they were mistaken – my heart makes no mistake:
For every single corpse I see, my brother's face will take.

Translated from the German by **Michael Gittins.**

Paula Ludwig (1900-1974)

Born in Austria, Paula Ludwig was uprooted many times. In 1940 she began exile in Brazil due to the rise of Nazism, returning to Europe in the early 1950s. In 1963 she was awarded the Georg Trakl Prize. The German original of the 1932 collection, re-issued in 2015, was first published as *Dem dunklen Gott. Ein Jahresgedicht der Liebe. Verlag C.H.Beck, München* (formerly: *Langewiesche-Brandt, Ebenhausen bei München*), and is translated by kind permission of the publishers.

To the Dark God

(1)
On the widened shore of the sea
I was left behind,
Lamenting the flood
That the sea had brought me
And inexorably took away again.

But perhaps it is only this
That a lifetime is not enough
To wait
For its return.

(2)
Where is the friend
Searching for me in the flower gardens
Over there
Where only the door groans in the breeze
That I
When I left, alas,
Forgot to shut.

(3)
Always I listen out
If there is no one to call me.

Like a window
Incessantly drenched
With rain running down
My face lies
Under my tears.

(4)
Oh, the wildest blossom of the wilderness
Smiled for me

Oh, the darkest tress of darkness
Slept with me:

Oh, let me never forget
How wonderful it was

When grief over-shadowed
What no longer exists.

(5)
In the evening the pink hyacinth
Began to release her sweet scent
And irresistibly her soul streamed away.

She never returned to her faded blossoms.

But who of us lamented this –

Rapturously we remember her
Only to say
Oh how unforgettably sweet
The scent of the pink hyacinth that evening.

Translated from the German by **Wilf Deckner**

Anonymous

This Anglo-Saxon elegy was written around the 8th or 9th century.

Ruin

Wondrous stones, *wyrde* has broken
our city; the work of giants is smashed –
roofs are fallen, towers ruined.
The frosted gate bitten into by rime
is off its hinges, ravaged and destroyed
by age's undertones. Earth has taken
the almighty builders, departed and decaying
in grave's grip, until a hundred life-
spans of men are gone. This wall –
red-stained and lichened through one
kingdom after another – stood under
storms; steep and tall, it is fallen.

The masonry, warped by weather,
grim, ground down,
                                    mud-crusted.
Iron rings bind foundations
cleverly constructed,
by a wise man,
                            wire-welded.

O bright buildings, nobly gabled,
bath houses, the racket of soldiers,
a multitude of mead halls, dreams
and drama, fate has swiped you flat.
Slaughter felled us, plague came,
all were slain by the great swordsman.
The temple idols murdered, their places
of war collapsed, rebuilders perished
beside shrines. Halls are empty, desolate,
their vaulted roofs, devoid of tiles,

brought to the ground.
                    Riven to rubble
on a gold morning, where happy men,
gleaming in sunlight, glittering, vain,
flushed on wine, bright in armour,
gazed on treasure, silver and jewels.

On capital, ownership and precious stones,
on the bright castle of a rich kingdom.
Buildings stood by a hot stream,
winding, wide-flowing to where a wall
held all within its bosom.

                    Baths burning
at the core, offering easy warmth,
the water's roar;

                    gushing over stones
under the encircling pool, steaming,
were that noble thing.
                    How once the city…

Version translated using various sources by **Lynn Foote**

Kristin Dimitrova (1963-)

Is a Bulgarian writer and poet, winner of five national awards for
poetry, three for prose and one for the translation of John Donne's
poetry into Bulgarian. This translation was produced in collaboration
with the author and with her permission.

In the Motley Din

The mute trumpets
of the petunias on the terrace
have unfurled in sensational poses.
Gorged with incongruous pink
from the soil, all of them

are welcoming summer.
On the longest day
air is a rare commodity,
the sun will torment us
until gone midnight.
From time to time
Fate gives us chocolate milk
so we don't whine.
Yes, I love you too -
she says - hush now,
I have something important to finish.

And I stay hushed. And I'm glad
what's important is far away.

Translated from the Bulgarian by **Tom Phillips**

Johann Wolfgang von Goethe (1749-1832)

Goethe is believed to have written the *Wanderer's Nightsong II (Über allen Gipfeln)* on September 6, 1780, onto the wall of a gamekeeper lodge on top of the Kickelhahn mountain where he passed the night. It is set to music by Franz Schubert, in 1823, Op. 96 No. 3, D. 768.

Wanderer's Nightsong

O'er every mountain-top
Rest lies,
In every tree-top
Sighs
The merest breeze.
Birdsong fades in the woodland gloom.
Just wait, and soon
Your pain shall ease.

Translated from the German by **Michael Gittins**

Emilie Jelinek

The Big Bang Theory

states that
the branches of the oak are still bare
though the blackthorn is fading
and April ends at midnight.
A single point of nothingness
also known as a singularity
lies within every closed bud,
so compact it has no dimension.
Suddenly – and no one quite knows why –
a stream of mist pours over
marshland where a swan
guards her universe-shaped eggs
and the silvered pilgrimage
of a snail lights up new leaves.
Tune into that weird static
between stations, the fine-
grain detail: the moment
our future was flung out across the void.

Roger Camp

A Flight of Lanterns

A crown canopy of Chinese Lanterns
floats above my head,
tiger-eyed swirls twisting
salt-water taffy in the breeze,
the bush-tits crazily clinging to their sides
on their comic carnival ride,
pecking clean stems and caps green.

Duncan Forbes

Mrs Mortimer's Podcast

Men? Flowers don't have much choice
when it comes to bees, do they?
Children. You get what you're given
and as for the virgin birth. Try it.
The root cause of all this extinction rebellion
and global warming is over-population
and over-copulation.
It's not as if there's no birth-control.
It's no self-control to the power of n.
Marie Stopes must be turning in her grave.
I'm going to be cremated and one of my
feckless sons can jolly well scatter my ashes
in Torbay or wherever. I hope he gets some of me
in his eye. Dying? No, I'm not afraid of it.
Everyone else has died so far, haven't they?
As for money, it's lovely to have enough lolly.
To have grown old and not be poor,
that's a real aspiration worth having.
Dr Bramble is hopeless with ingrown toenails
and don't ask me what a defibrillator is.
There's one outside the village stores
but I wouldn't know how to work it anyway.
The Bible has a lot to answer for,
so does the Koran. Unreadable, for a start.
As for Genesis, can you imagine any male making
heaven and earth and all that therein is?
Most of them can't even make a bed properly.
I can't dress like a super-model anymore.
When you've got one foot in the grave,
you've got to have comfortable footwear.
It's the resurrection of the dead

which scares the living daylights out of me,
not that I believe in any of that malarkey.
Imagine meeting all those revitalised corpses.
It's such a stupid superstition.
Try saying that quickly and with dentures.

Catherine Baker

Self Portrait as a Cutlery Drawer

The splintered love-spoon with half a heart
is pushed to the back with a silver tea strainer
and nutmeg grater, rusty. There's a wooden
borscht spoon stained purple and a pair of
chopsticks wrapped in faded rice paper.
Skewers for barbecues, bought in Tasmania.
The knives are mainly stainless steel, blunt
or slyly serrated and will snick unwary fingers.
A soft green one has a rabbit handle and milk
tooth indentations. There are forks, of course,
some with tines out of alignment and two are
dainty and superfluous, meant for eating cakes.
A miscellany of spoons clumps and will clink
alarmingly if the drawer is opened unwarily.
Serving spoons for dollops of greek yogurt
or baked beans. Some, inscribed GWR, are
humpbacked after a competition of teenage
might. There are teaspoons for Calpol,
turmeric and Canderel, a champagne cork
(Bollinger), a few dead flies, a hair slide, crumbs,
a menu for Thai takeaway and a rubbery thing,
circular and sticky for gripping truculent jars
if I ever find anything impossible to open.

Chris Hardy

Sermon on Mount Helikon

Blessed are the poets for they celebrate the daisy and the stone
for they remember the unnamed and forgotten
for they betray confession
for they embroider life with names
for they listen on the bus
for they wear a coat of words
for they audit an abacus of trees
for they heed the butterfly of Lefka Ori

Blessed are the poets for they eavesdrop on God and nothing
for they change their tongue
for they walk beneath the sea
for they read a dish of celery
for they place silence above light
for they assess homunculus and poltergeist
for they regret Aleppo
for they attend the other side of Pluto

Blessed are the poets for they skry death and birth
for they climb to Hesiod's hearth
for they speak with the pavement cat
for they encompass cumulus and Oort
for they find love in a laundry basket
for they fathom water
for they respect hate and fear
for they sit by the fountain in the square

J.S. Watts

Monkey Night at the Circus

Monkey see.
Monkey do.
Monkey gone.
No longer my monkey.
No longer my circus.
Say goodbye to the red haired clowns,
the tension, the drama, the spangled tears.
No more balancing on an impossible wire,
spinning dizzily up high with no way down,
the world running round and round like it will never stop,
everything smooth and shiny bright,
its surface sticky with blurred rainbows.
I sleep better now at night, but the dark sparkles less.

I liked the way the yearning circus lights always
shimmered across the sequins and the glitter,
wishing on a thousand twinkly stars,
pink and gold and bleeding-heart red.
The air stuffed full of the warm sweet banquet-promise
of candyfloss and popcorn.
The crazy, ginger clown made me laugh as well as cry
and the performing monkeys with
their tiny, clever hands and winning grins,
those curling, gripping, funny tails
that wrapped around your fingers
as if they wanted to hold on forever.
I miss the monkeys.

Jonathan Steffen

Portuguese Churches

They tower on the hilltops of the far Reconquest,
Holding up their crosses to the heavens –
Tall centuries of flinty faith
Piled high to fill the sky with their conviction.
Once new, once bright, once bold,
They groan now under their own history,
Amassing moss, and scaffolding, and tourists,
While from the altar steps the Word is read aloud
To generations of vacant pews.
When did the certainty ebb from these holy halls
To spend itself amongst the pigeons and the traffic
And the windswept squares below?
Perhaps one day the church bell tolled
A little less insistently than usual,
And the choir sang out a little less brightly,
And the incense hung a touch less thickly on the air,
Then suddenly, on a day like any other,
A day of wind and pigeons and an almost empty sky,
Someone looked up at them,
And saw them as they were,
Aloft and alone and abandoned –
Just as we were one day to realize
That the house of our great love
Was actually standing cold and empty,
With its tiles falling from the rooftop,
And the paint peeling from the window-frames,
And the front door yawning open on its hinges
To welcome in some curious stranger.

Sue Spiers

Man, Aged and Brown
After Pablo Neruda

Man, aged and brown, the sun that freckles
your skin, that fades your cap, that wilts orchids,
covers your body with melanoma, and your sea grey eyes
and your mouth that has the grin of the fox.

A dark, malevolent sun is twisted into skeins
of your white hair, when you lengthen your stride
you walk in shadows as with a thick novel
which leaves the ending uncertain.

Man, aged and brown, life draws me away from you.
everything takes me further as though you were night.
You are the wizened bloom of the passion flower,
the intoxication of milk, the strength of the humming bird.

My melancholy heart waits for you, achingly,
and I love your frail body, your hesitant voice.
Slow caterpillar, tentative and careful
like the fallow field and the moth, the thistle and the wind.

Jonathan Steffen

My Bravest Brindle

Lie long, my bravest brindle:
Leap lightly in your deepest dreams.
All pain will pass, all sorrow cease,
And all the agonies of age will lift and leave at last,
Like geese upon the greying, silent sky.

H.D. AFTER IMAGISM:

Fred Beake

H.D., the American poet Hilda Doolittle (1886–1961), while still in her late twenties and early thirties, with some help from Ezra Pound and her husband Richard Aldington, made a name for herself as *H.D. Imagiste* in the literary worlds of London and America about the time of the First World War, with both her poetry and editing. She became a leading member of the imagist grouping that included Williams, Pound and others. Her major achievement of this period was the 1916 book *Sea Garden*. Its strange, intense dreamlike poems drifted fragmentedly across a world out of Ancient Greece. Thus from *the Wind Sleepers*.

> We no longer sleep
> in the wind –
> we awoke and fled
> through the city gate.
>
> Tear –
> tear us an altar,
> tug at the cliff boulders...

The poems also mirror present reality with their excursions among the strange fauna of the sea shore. Thus from *Sea Lily*.

> Myrtle-bark
> is flecked from you,
> scales are dashed from your stem,
> sand cuts your petal,…:

Swinburne, Shelley and Tennyson had explored a dream world out of Ancient Greece before H.D. but this was totally different. To use a musical analogy, H.D.'s imagist poems are more like Debussy piano pieces than Beethoven or Schubert sonatas. The awareness of nature as a hostile, daemonic force, which had some closeness to D.H. Lawrence, who corresponded with H.D. and was influenced by her, set her apart from most of her contemporaries; even Edward Thomas is inclined to see nature more benignly than H.D.

However, there was a distinct change to H.D.'s work after her marriage to Aldington broke up in the middle of World War I and she had a child by the composer Cecil Grey. Then she nearly died of

Spanish Flu from which she was rescued by Bryher, who got her in to hospital at the critical moment. Bryher was the illegitimate daughter of the shipping magnate, Sir John Ellerman. As a child she was very boyish and lively and realized she was lesbian very young. She adopted the name by which she was universally known from one of the Scilly Isles. She was also a young poet of the imagist school, who sought H.D. out because she admired her poetry. Bryher was never that successful as a poet, though she was to become a not undistinguished writer of historical novels and a fine autobiographer in later life. Thanks to having a wealthy shipping magnate as a father she was the generous supporter of numerous literary and artistic ventures, notably the magazine *Life and Letters Today*. That apart she was H.D.'s companion and protector from 1919 on and the provider of considerable financial support, not least for the analysis by Freud that was to lead to H.D.'s fine book about that experience, *Tribute to Freud*. And the fact that Bryher always looked after H.D.'s needs and expected her to write meant that H.D. poured out book after book.

After these events the poems tended to lose their imagist terseness and become arguably less inspired and looking for acceptable Greek subjects, rather than waiting for them to emerge. There is no huge decline in the second half of H.D.'s 1925 Collected Poems. However, there is just enough after *Sea Garden's* successor *The Pool* to make you see why the 1925 *Collected* must have marked a point for H.D. at which poetry ceased to be her main priority for nearly twenty years.

She turned to prose shortly after meeting Bryher and a new method of writing seems to develop in the novel *Hedylus* and the three novellas of *Palimpsest* from the early twenties. There is some presence of Robert Browning and even perhaps the Victorian historical novel in these mirrors of the Greek, Roman and Modern worlds, but viewed through the stream of consciousness of Virginia Wolf and others and full of intense awareness of detail, which is not unrelated to those marvellously visual moments in *Sea Garden* and *the Pool*. Thus from Palimpsest, 'The very room she gazed at seemed the old and frayed out image of some nightmare. Superimposed still was this crystal water, ice green from which gazed Hipparchia'. Compare with *Oread* from *The Pool*.

> Whirl up, sea —
> whirl your pointed pines,
> Splash your great pines

on our rocks,
hurl your green over us,
cover us with your pools of fir.

H.D. was not only turning away from the imagism of her youth. She and Bryher, despite periodic returns to London had effectively left England, where H.D. had done such outstanding work in just half a dozen years, and were wandering about Europe, taking advantage of Bryher's wealth. This inevitably meant that H.D., though not wholly forgotten in literary London, did become distanced from it. However, in 1923 it also took H.D. to Karnak where she came into contact with the people and gods of Ancient Egypt. This was to play a large part in her writing . She and Bryher used Switzerland as an alternative home and established something approaching a bi commune, as may be glimpsed in that fine H.D. novel, *Nights,* from the thirties. But remember also her daughter's comment that "Mercifully H.D. laughed a great deal... She had, and was, fun." It was also a world where Bryher's fascination with modern psychoanalysis for her friends and companions must have been creative in causing H.D. search her inner self, though also perhaps a touch oppressive.

Even by the standards of the Roaring Twenties, the two women's love life was tangled. Bryher, in 1927, married H.D.'s main male lover, Kenneth Macpherson. Silent film was in the two women's lives before Macpherson, whose chief interest was in film, but his presence made it even more so. *Borderline,* the film that he made more or less in collaboration with H.D. and Bryher, is well worth seeing (The British Film Institute has a copy). It has a sadness, of strangers not fitting in, such as the character played by the American bass baritone, Paul Robeson. However, despite Robeson's presence, it is H.D's extraordinary face and presence that dominate. You get a feeling of her character that I find more real than anything in the many writings about her.

It seems probable that after 1919 the silent films of the day affected H.D.'s writing as much as the fashionable literary stream of consciousness. H.D. shifted from the single intense imagist moments of *Sea Garden* and *The Pool* into a world where multiple moments drift into one another in a film-like way. This is especially true of her great poems of the forties and fifties, *Trilogy*, *Helen in Egypt,* the three sequences of *Hermetic Definition,* and the final poem, *Winter Love*, which are the height of her achievement after 1925.

This film-like quality, this drifting of moments into something larger is equally true of the very fine *Asphodel,* begun in 1921-2. Whether Asphodel is a novel or a prose poem is a good question, either way it is one of H.D.'s finest books and the first of several attempts to come to terms with her complex sexuality before 1920. Curiously, she never attempted to publish *Asphodel,* but subsumed much of its material into the later novels *Bid Me to Live* and *HERmione. Asphodel* is the first and one of the finest examples of this method of single moments eliding into a larger whole, which affected both her prose and poetry.

H.D. grew up reading the Victorian poets. When she was young and lonely in Philadelphia during the 1900s before her escape to London, the pre-Raphaelites and Browning mattered to her; Swinburne was a beacon of sexual and poetic rebellion as he was for many other young people at the time. While Browning and Swinburne do not break their longer poems up into separate moments like H.D. does in her later work, nevertheless they attack the same problem of how to keep a long poem driving forward. Indeed, at the end of her life when she was briefly stuck for a way forward she re-read Swinburne and wrote the very fine *Winter Love* in 1959. She wrote to her great ally, the American academic (and Wartime intelligence officer), Norman Holmes Pearson, 'Some of the poems are done in a strangely familiar, Swinburnian meter – I can't think that I *must* be Pound-Eliot.'

The thirties produced the novel *Nights,* which was one of H.D.'s finest achievements. Otherwise it was a difficult period for her creatively. She undoubtedly found the coming of the Nazis oppressive and was beginning the struggle to turn the material of *Asphodel* into something perhaps more acceptable and less radical in what became eventually *HERmione* and *Bid Me to Live.*

When war was obviously coming in 1939 Bryher would have much preferred to stay in Switzerland, where, as she wryly points out in her autobiography *The Days of Mars,* the authorities had laid in ample and good quality food and stores against the country being cut off in a major war, in marked contrast to England. However, H.D. had other ideas; she wanted to be in London as she had been in World War One and where she had written her best poems; and she made her way there, more or less in spite of Bryher. Bryher made a late and rather perilous arrival via Portugal well into 1940, so late indeed that Osbert

Sitwell was supposed to have remarked that he was rather expecting her to arrive with the German invasion barges.

H.D. and Bryher lived together in a flat while the war raged over London, enduring the poor rations that went with living in a British city during World War Two. Bryher involved herself a good deal with the magazine *Life and Letters Today*. H.D. no doubt was glad to be quite near her daughter Perdita, who was old enough to take a small part in the war. She was also much occupied with explorations of the occult, not least the possibilities of contacting the dead. She took part in many sessions that are to some extent recorded (with some fictionalisation) in her book *Majic Ring* and the occult novel *The Sword Went Out To Sea*. Her belief was genuine and the many references among those who knew her to H.D.'s lively and down to earth sense of humour and frequent laughter offset suggestions that she was unbalanced, as indeed does the careful lively observation of her short stories from this period. Her belief that she was in contact with R.A.F. pilots who had died in the Battle of Britain led to exchanges with Lord Dowding, the retired commander of R.A.F. Fighter Command, who had interests in the occult. As Lord Howell he appears in the *Sword Went Out To Sea*.

Much more important is the enormous step forward that the three sequences of *Trilogy* represent. In their very different way they are as important as the *Four Quartets*, which are roughly contemporary. They are the first major poetry H.D. had written since *The Pool* in 1918. Their context is perhaps best described in a 1943 letter to Norman Holmes Pearson, '...starved, suffocated – flung from our raft on the beleaguered rock– "this England" – or the rock of latter-day falsity and laisser-aller, the between-wars I mean...That is how it is – and too, in the fifty thousand incidents of the actual Blitz." The free verse paragraphs of irregular length of H.D.'s previous poetry are abandoned in favour of two line couplets (except in the very first poem, which is in three lines). Having 43 sub sections to each of the three parts no doubt gave direction to these constantly shifting meditations. The poems need to be read and re-read with an open mind. Part one begins:

> An incident here and there,
> and rails gone (for guns)
> from your (and my) old town square;

> mist and mist-grey, no colour,
> still the Luxor bee, chick and hare
> pursue unalterable purpose
>
> in green, rose-red, lapis;
> they continue to prophesy
> from the stone papyrus…

But how to re-enter the Ancient Wisdom when 'Evil was active in the land' and the ancient Goddess, whether '…Isis, Aset, Astarte is a harlot…' Yet the caduceus, the healing rod of the ancients, can still flower. These arguments with many variations run through the 43 sections of part one till finally '…the floor sags/ like a ship floundering;/ we know no rule of procedure,…/ we have no map; possibly we will reach haven, heaven.'

Memories of the *Book of Revelation* and its seven angels are important to the second part. After all, an apocalyptic war is happening in the real world. Nonetheless, the second half of part two becomes increasingly joyful as the female goddess is invoked:

> We have seen her
> the world over, …
>
> We have seen her, an empress,
> magnificent in pomp and grace,
>
> and we have seen her
> with a single flower
>
> or a cluster of garden pinks
> in a glass beside her…

Part three builds on this, using a story of Kaspar and Mary Magdalene. Kaspar gives the jar of myrrh that Mary Magdalene gives to Christ. The writing is exhilarating. Perhaps the culmination is in 37:

> And as the snow fell on Hebron,
> the desert blossomed as it had always done;
>
> over-night, a million-million tiny plants
> broke from the sand,
>
> and a million-million little grass-stalks
> each put out a tiny flower, …

In 1946 H.D. was taken seriously ill. It is still an open question whether this was cerebral meningitis, possibly due to poor wartime diet as said at the time, or mental health issues resulting from the occult explorations, as Barbara Guest wrote in her questionable biography in the eighties. H.D. was transferred by Bryher to a clinic in Switzerland, where she made a fairly rapid recovery, working on *The Sword Went Out to Sea* in 1947. She spent the rest of her life in Switzerland till her death in 1961, in and out of various clinics. Bryher continued to be H.D.'s protector, but the relationship effectively ceased.

This was an enormously creative period. The poem *Helen in Egypt* uses the myth that the Gods whisked Helen away from Troy to Egypt and substituted an image of her during the Trojan War to explore all the stories about Helen in a unique way. The book is haunted by H.D.'s own life, which possibly provides the poem's considerable force. As with *Borderline,* H.D.'s remarkable recording of the poem gives a strong feeling of her presence. The three sequences of *Hermetic Definition* explore H.D.'s inner life and courage in the face of life winding down. Finally *Winter Love* is more Helen poems, but more lyrical and in some ways more surreal than *Helen in Egypt*. To me it always seems more a new beginning than an ending, as good as anything H.D. ever wrote:

> The golden apples of the Hesperides,
> the brushed bloom of the pollen,
> on the wing of ravishing butterfly or plundering bee;
>
> the gold of evanescence or the gold
> of heavy-weighted treasure,
> which will out-weigh the other?
>
> grandam, great *Grande Dame,*
> we will go on together ,
> and find the way to hyacinths by a river,
>
> where a harp-note sounded
> and a moment later –
> grandam, great *Grande Dame*, He is here with us,
>
> in notes ascending and descending from his lyre,
> your Child, my Child and Helios' Child, no other,
> to lure us on, on, on, Euphorion, *Espérance.*

Chris Rice

White Dog Waking

The room is quiet, no longer filled with trombone
snores and hiccupped dreams of chasing Lycra-
vested locusts racing bikes in Richmond Park;
Morris dancers celebrating May Day in Rye Harbour …

She stretches, yawns and sits up at the bottom
of my bed, floppy ears of ginger silk, pink tongue
lolling like a carpet from a missing staircase;
kohl-lashed, toffee-apple eyes watching

from a twitching hairy meadow of moustaches
for me to wake from dreams of wolves in
medieval forests. Sunrise through the curtains
turns a white dog waking on my blanket pink.

Jenny Hamlett

Masked

Too early and unsteady
I walk slowly along the half-empty corridor.
My glasses steam as I breathe,
blotting out direction signs and leaving me
stranded in a boat without oars.

What has happened to me?
What has happened to the alert,
making a joke of my hearing,
proud of my lip reading, me?

I fumble my way to a receptionist.
She says something. I hesitate.
She points towards some chairs.
I sit, get up and go back. *Sorry,*
I say, *I'm deaf. I won't hear the call.*

I think it must have worked.
A figure in grey
hospital uniform shuffles forward.

I follow him, hoping
this is the right thing to do.
We enter a smaller area.
The man speaks. I hesitate,
look towards the changing rooms.

He says something angry and points
to a hard, red plastic chair.

I'm out of my depth, sit hunched
and silent over my bag.
At a distance, a tough-looking youth,
in trench coat and thick black mask
removes it for a few seconds.

He says, *They don't understand.*
The rope he's swung towards me holds.
Thanking him I smile, hoping
he can see it in my eyes,
and scramble ashore;
the shreds of my identity holding hands.

Samantha Carr

Moon Landing

Some say that it was a hoax,
but I remember every moment
of when The Men arrived. They
set down their craft upon my
soft craters. No permission
to land requested. Claimed me
as though a flag could limit
the gravity of my moonlight. A
crescent shaped teardrop, as
they took small steps across my
skin. Creeping, entering and taking
pleasure in knowing that they
were on me. The scars remain
although they blasted off as quick
as they came. My orbit wary of
incoming as they watch me at night.

David Callin

Out of the Past

This is the doubtful hour. Shapes start
to flow into each other. Shades
creep out from under trees, where they've
avoided the dogmatic sun
all day, to gather with their friends.

This is the time of day when things
are seen to be believed. The light,
more diffident, obliquer, drops
its flat insistence on who's who
and joins us in the masquerade.

Now, if ever, I will meet
my father in his Sunday best,
with the light behind him, walking
out of those old photographs,
their cracked duns and ochres,

or – more disheveled – looking shyly
over his shoulder as he backs
a tractor out of some tight spot,
tinkering with a motor-bike
or posing with a euphonium

we never saw, likewise the bike;
nor do we recognise this farmhouse
with its sycamores and sorry
garden, or this pretty girl
who sits, smiling, in a hedge.

W.D. Jackson

Aesopean

A poor wild ass inquired of his friend,
A donkey, *how* he'd grown so plump.
The donkey grinned. But his backbone was bent
From the stones he had to hump.

The ass, sneering, chewed a dry thistle.
That night a starving pack
Of hyenas chewed *him*, skin and gristle.
The donkey rested his back.

William Virgil Davis

Journey

I step into my shadow
and the shadow goes away.

How many blackbirds
are sitting in that tree?

If snow fell sideways
would the flakes spin or stop?

Old cats eat slowly.

The colour I most want to inherit
is blue, colour of clouds and water.

When fog obscures the trees beside the lake,
boats disappear, are never seen again.

An evening like this
is one in a million.

Can you see where we are going?

Responses

Dear *Acumen*

I was delighted to read Patricia's article in Acumen on Gerard Manley Hopkins. I was given a copy of his selected poems and prose when I was 17. It was already well-used but is now very battered indeed! It has accompanied me through many of life's experiences and the concept and reality of inscape has become key to the way I look at the physical world and its reverberations in all other dimensions.

Also fascinating was the interview with Seán Street and his connections with radio, a medium that I've enjoyed throughout my adult life for its intimacy. I was reminded that a group once visited CB1 poetry at the café in Mill Road, Cambridge, explaining the practice of Radio Poetry, which appeared to be the gathering of random words from the radio and the creation of poems from these. I wasn't entirely convinced that it made sense to me but then again, not all poems make sense on every level but do work on the senses nevertheless.

The Poems in Translation proved an excellent bunch, very much including Peter Eagles' essay and translations of Osip Mandelstam.

Trish Harewood, Cambridgeshire

Dear *Acumen*,

Congratulations on such a good number 102. The article on Hopkins sent me back to some of my favourite poems by him. I also appreciated new poems by Kevin Higgins, Michael Swan, Diane Hendry, Niall McGrath and Jane Newberry among many others. The reviews too were interesting and informative.

David Ball, France

Dear *Acumen*,

I'm just writing to let you know how much I enjoyed Peter Eagles's article about the Voronezh poems of Osip Mandelstam in Acumen 102.

I received an impression of great austerity and purity which I found very inspiring and which somehow seemed to create a connection to the true roots of poetry – the roots of reality, in other words.

Polly Walshe, Oxford

Obituary: Francis Warner

Francis Warner, poet, dramatist and academic died in Oxford on December 7th 2021. He was a great supporter of *Acumen* – he bought several copies of every issue, one for himself and others to give to friends and students.

He studied English (at both undergraduate and postgraduate level) in Cambridge, after previously studying at the London College of Music. His postgraduate supervisor, C.S. Lewis, described him as "a promising scholar and the best-mannered man of his generation". In 1965 he came to St. Peter's College, Oxford as Fellow in English Literature. I was one of his first tutees. He was an inspiring teacher, generous with his time, his knowledge, ideas and books. He published less scholarly work than he might have done, given his wide-ranging learning – regarding teaching as the more important activity. He did, however, write and publish a substantial body of poems and plays. Most of his poetry (some of which appeared in *Acumen*) was in traditional forms though, as in *Experimental Sonnets* (1965), he often handled them in new ways. *Collected Poems:1960-1984* was published in 1985. Further volumes of poetry followed, but much of his attention switched to the stage. His early plays, such as *Lying Figures* (1972) and *Killing Time* (1976) were rigorously experimental. They were followed by a sequence of blank-verse dramas, studies in the interplay of Christian and Classical, the relationships between patrons and artists and between powerful men and the women loved by them; highlights include *Healing Nature: The Athens of Pericles* (1988), *Virgil and Caesar* (1998) and *Rembrandt's Mirror* (2000).

Francis Warner had a great gift for friendship, whether with the famous (his friends included Samuel Beckett, Henry Moore, Richard Burton and Kathleen Raine) or with his current and former students. He was a good judge of character; he introduced me to my future wife, saying "I think you two will get on". We shall shortly celebrate our Golden Wedding anniversary.

Glyn Pursglove

Emma Lee

Fashionable Samba

Rose Ayling-Ellis & Giovanni Pernice dance a samba to Kate Hudson's "Cinema Italiano" , BBC's "Strictly Come Dancing"

The audience cannot clap while she dances.
Not hearing is the art of anticipation,
what might someone say, what an actor
might mean, what a director implies
by what's revealed through a lens
and what's left out. A fashion student
knows style may gloss over a faulty seam,
sequins deflect a misaligned pleat,
the wrong footwear can break an outfit.
Anticipation begins with figuring out a narrative,
building a story so not hearing each
individual word is not so crucial.
The cognitive focus is like a spell
easily broken by an interruption:
vibrations from a camera click,
an audience clap on the wrong beat.
She says she'll take her boots home.

Colin Pink

Triumphal Arch

Stone trumpet blaring across the city,
ragged now, pocked, like old skin.

Still boasting, brazen, making off with
the loot, dragging captives, the vanquished.

Purposeless, just to be ridden through
but chained off now, not even useful

to shelter under from a sudden shower
as we try to decipher the victor's name.

A chiselled attempt at immortality
now weathered, blurred, barely legible.

A stranger blurts random obscenities,
shooting automatic words. Am I in the way?

Vic Pickup

In Churchill's

The boy in the fish and chip shop
once felt sad enough to slice
the soft white skin
on the inside of his wrist.

He has a thick scar
shining wide and purple
like a fat worm sliding up his sleeve.
You'll see a flash of it

as he deftly shovels and shakes
the shimmering fish and chips
in air that sparkles
with hot oil spit
and running salt.

He hands me three warm bundles,
each triple-wrapped
with thick folds
neatly tucked.

Jo Haslam

The Speaking Tube

Your mother has taken the tube from her throat
and left it to soak overnight in a glass of cold water.
The metal still holds the print of her fingers,
the glass is filmed with her breath.
When she touches the hole at her neck
her voice is released as a hiss
or croak. It's a struggle to put the tube in
and sometimes she *can't be bothered.*
Her *speaking tube* she says, as if her voice
had a life of its own, as if it might whistle
or break into song, as if it might wake in the night
and call to her – *Annie, Annie* –
and she'd have to hush it quiet.
But now she mouths the words, as she did in the mill
when she couldn't be heard over the clack
of the looms; when she longed to be out
on the moor, when her voice could carry
over the wind and blown grass, when she could call
to her sister, her friends, when she could sing,
Barbary Allen, Molly Malone, Annie Laurie.

R.A. Zafar

Cracks

Like a row of graves
the shrunken pots of paint
line the windowsill
each one sits on a pale strip
painted by you.

You asked me too many times
what shade I wanted
for our naked bedroom
all the colours looked the same.

Your favourite was eggshell white –
you said you liked the name
as much as the colour
the white matched your parched paper skin
at the end.

If you had stopped spurning mirrors
you would have seen
you would have laughed
at your matching eggshell
(I imagine you would have laughed).

Now there is no decision to make
I carry you with me wherever I go:
left pocket – paint pot,
right pocket – your compact mirror –
its glassy lid cloudy and cool
in my palm.

I open your mirror every day
I want to catch you looking back
all I capture are pockmarked walls
and hairline cracks –

I keep trying to paint over them
every single one of them
with eggshell white.

Owen Gallagher

'And Yourself?'

'Donegal,' I say.

I see the stone and oak pier,
Inishboffin, Inishdooey and Tory Island,
seals sunbathing on the sandbanks,
the sky, blue as a Greek door.

I imagine you carrying me, in a hold-all
across the dunes to Falcarragh Strand,
and then clutching my urn tight,
you, my love, shake my ashes out

onto the clear icy water.
I am swept out and back, bits of me
here and there, until I'm spread
across the bay, floating, waving.

'Fine,' you say.

Sandra Fulton

Sea-Roads

I have come to talk to you
Because the days draw in
And because I can hear the sea –
The distant, long sigh of it.
I hear the gull-cry.
But mostly, I hear the sea.

And, farthest of all, the thunder
The ominous deep dirge of it:
A shape on the mind's horizon,
The drumming of a dream-rider.
But it is coming.

So I have come to talk to you
Of the days that run downhill
With the rain-seasons to the sea,
And of the road that follows.
You must understand.

Alex Walker

Strange Winter

river pouring
daily puff of coal
chatter of friends
press of water against the lock gates
overflow
balsamic moon
I am swallowed up
I am swept away in the overflow
of turkey tails lobular expanses
drops of rain strung like beads of liquid starlight
gathering the essence of trees
the inconceivable wisdom of lichen
the blinding luminescence of mossy fingers
'chuckle chuckle' slurs the river
and I cling on
to myself with these words
in this day full of life
full of the tides turning
sap rising
seeds bursting deep in the soil

Maggie Freeman

Chainsaw

It has algal disease, said the stranger
with the chainsaw, astride the lawn in his yellow
chain-link suit, of the tree
with meagre and bitter fruit
whose trunk when I pushed it with one finger
leaned alarmingly.
Cut it down then, I said.

When darkness fell, indoors
my finger traced a glass screen
for algal disease in apples.
Nothing. This thing has a shape
I can't put a true name to
but still the stranger from the road
has cut up my worry and taken it away
in the back of his pick-up.

There is now this space in the garden, and light
and all day I have laboured to fill
the bare earth around the stump
with plants that will flower and grow tall
and bright, and flourish. I carry cans
of water to nourish them.

Matthew Smith

Rose Unknown

Without a name, it turns
in the garden as you walk.
Burns in air, like mind
underwater: surfaces glitter.

Something like fragrance stirs.
Open heart. Petals fall.
Dewdrops rest on red, stars at dawn.

Pauline Hawkesworth

Farlington Marshes

Spent the day wave-walking
to the small oyster house
just off the shore.
The crisp white shells
layered and pressed,
form book leaves that tell
of neglect.
My feet stub rubble and decay.

Locked into its furthest corners
where lapwings bob and gulls
swarm, empty shorelines
are transformed into submerged
grandeur, taking with them sights
and sounds of birds and people.

Pottery crushed pebbles
are sharp, almost new.
Upturned stones reveal creatures
struggling to remain anonymous.
They and I stroke each other.
And whether storms shout
or my voice raises itself,
no-one will come.
This is the forgotten place
where humans exercise
primitive beliefs.

Sheila Spence

How to know a bumblebee

Try to draw

each golden stripe
and silver-veined wing
each jointed leg and claw,

the furry bee-ness of it
busy on sun-drenched lavender.

Listen

to the bombination
and buzz of it

 its hum

and hear the voice
of summer.

Gina Wilson

Somewhere to Live

I like the way this privet
stands its ground,
the waist-high lavender,
crazy paving,
tubs.

These winter trees, that never touch,
remind me of Mother and the Aunts,
how, in the end, I felt their twigs,
like children's fingers,
tug.

I want to join again with buds, bees,
swing upside down with apples,
wave at grass –
watch how it weaves itself
like straw,
ready to catch me
if I fall.

Avaughan Watkins

The Beekeeper

She is veiled, white gowned,
holding by its neck
a metal rooster that clucks with smoke.
Under the cottage cheese blossom
there's a fae circle of wooden homes.
With a gloved hand
she snaps the propolis
under the gabled roof; a behemoth bride
revealing a giant's causeway of honeycomb
capped with cream,

a trove of bees
and some sing like coins.
She scrapes away old wax chalices
and eventually finds her queen –
her autumn pinecone back
her embroidered, onyx eyes.

When she returns, I kiss her lips
and feel the chant of their wings
I smell the sleeping ash
and taste the sweetness of gold.

Stuart Handysides

Somewhere Still To Go

My father knew his time was short
when ordering the plot, but even so
he would have liked his grave to face downhill
toward the town and morning sun.

My mother, on the day, refused to look
into the hole, dug deep, designed for two
– continued to deny that she would die.

I seldom visit: faded plastic flowers
and silk that's frayed suggest half-hearted care
that wouldn't really cut it if they knew.

But something in the place where less and less
remains of their remains retains its force,
a sense of having come from somewhere,
having somewhere still to go.

John Arnold

Silver Lady

Eleanor Thornton – model for "Spirit of Ecstasy", and the basis for the Rolls-Royce "silver lady" mascot – drowned from a torpedoed ship in 1915.

Poised
on the cusp
of ecstasy,

of a dive
into sunless depths,
her quicksilver body

sculpted in a gasp,
a sharp orgasm of light.
She leans

into the wind, leaps, plunges:
marbled in ocean shadow,
lost into legend.

Veronica Aaronson

Leaving Home

You're waving goodbye from the shore, smiling.

I want to get off the boat, but
the swell knocks me off balance and
with each heave away from you
I'm more seasick, homesick.
I call gently to you – *No fuss*, you'd said.
I whisper your name
to calm myself
as the distance between us widens. I try everything:
I wave your wave, smile your smile,
as if mirroring might bring us close again.

As if mirroring might bring us close again,
I wave your wave, smile your smile
as the distance between us widens. I try everything
to calm myself:
I whisper your name.
I call gently to you – *No fuss*, you'd said.
I'm more seasick, homesick.
with each heave away from you.
The swell knocks me off balance and
I want to get off the boat, but

you're waving goodbye from the shore, smiling.

Kris Spencer

Wrestling Cholitas

Inspired by the Cholitas of Bolivia, and the photographs of Todd Antony.

I stand behind my mother. She presses the pedal
and feeds the cloth, threading the levers
as the needle drops. She is an eagle in the ring.

Shouts to the crowd, *El que no corre… vuela –*
That which doesn't run… flies. Tells me her wings
are borrowed. I ask her, *What bird am I?*

Her layered skirts are mint and lemon; she wears
an orange shawl, embroidered with flowers. Says,
You will be pretty, take care. Plaits my hair.

I learn from my mother how I should fight. Her shining
braids are heavy as sugar. *Our hair is our glory and our*
history. She takes me with her, every Sunday. Buys me

a soda; I make it last two hours. In the ring, she cries out,
Lucho por el amor de mi padre – I fight for the love
of my father. Lets me move the wheel slowly as she turns

the cloth. *You are a kingfisher,* she tells me. When I grow
up my pollera will be orange, cyan and blue. I lie in bed
and watch. Up and down the needle goes as she runs a seam.

Daniel Boland

Poppies by the Sea

Orangey-red prayer flags of the past –
they are opium –
a secret incense.

They are a doorway to everything –
from a small room
to an endless blue seascape.

They launch all the people
that you have encountered –
the living and the dead.

They are the raw emotions
housed in your always changing body
unfurling now like a beautiful sail.

They all well up and churn on the waves.

They give visions of a solitary hosta plant
that made you think of the venerable Bede.

They are those curvy-stemmed flowers that grew
beside the red wagon you had as a child.

They gesture nervously
toward a pod of blue whales in the distance
as you draw
closer and closer to the shore
to the crashing surf
to the lighthouse.

Then back to the world.

REVIEWS

RUSSIAN AND BELARUSIAN VOICES SPEAKING FOR UKRAINE

In My Garden of Mutants by Volha Napeyeva, translated by Annie Rutherford. Arc Publications. 48pp.; £7.
Solar Eclipse 1914: Selected Poems by Arkseny Tarkovsky, translated by Peter Oram. Arc Publications. 84pp.; £10.99.

Since being asked to review these two bi-lingual texts last year, Russia's invasion of Ukraine has caused the world's tectonic plates to shift, sadly giving them a particular relevance. Volha Napayeva, an award-winning contemporary Belarusian poet, speaks out against state repression and the war that has, in fact, been ongoing for ten years in Eastern Ukraine, while the Soviet poet Arkseny Tarkovsky (1907-1989), as a Red Army war veteran and amputee, was well-qualified to write on the devastating effects of world wars, Stalin's purges and state control of dissident writers. It seems we are back where we started.

Thus, we no longer need the reminder in *In My Garden of Mutants*: "Volha's elliptical responses to the war in Ukraine offer a much closer perspective of this crisis at the edge of Europe than we often have the chance to encounter." Her work reinforces the distance between Russians and Belarusians and the acts of their leaders. In an intelligent, feisty yet richly nuanced voice she writes on individual rights, gender, nation, and language.

In her war poems, for example, the straight talking: "an unimportant day in history / for an unimportant people" ('13 October') is set beside a whole network of other war associations: innocently named weaponry, the cold neutrality of its effects, and memories of pre-war life. These all converge to condemn the aggressors and give a heartbreaking reinforcement of what has been lost: *"the factory is confident this new weapon / will find its consumer / … / butterfly mines / these fit in your palm / and weigh only 90 grams / like a newborn kitten / or a bar of soap / I weigh it in my hand // the bathroom is quiet and safe // trusting naivety // hyancinths, carnations and phloxes / blaze in the neighbour's yard"* (pp.35-37).

All her concerns, personal and political, converge to each person's right to their own space as part of their own culture, "determining the size // how much space I need for myself / how much for others" (p.41) but with a cynicism that doesn't hold out much hope of its realisation. Her richly layered snow imagery resonates painfully with what we have seen on our screens of the one and half million [as at the date of writing] currently forced across European borders:

> where snow falls today
> I will be absent
> where silence attempts a confession
> the intentions of others cannot be made out
> and you gaze for a long time at your impression in the glass
> picturing a short cut
> instead of your own long hair
> but you never pick up the scissors   (p.39)

One doesn't just flee from the bombardment but also from the subsequent loss of identity that occupation will bring – with hints of the gendered body that is explored widely in the collection. Snow then expands to represent a metaphysical sense of self: "so I go to the place where snow is born /… / promising nothing / he simply existed / being born and then dying."

The Belarusian language is movingly expressed in the final poem: "no matter who she asked, no one had heard of it / only one time somebody said / this word will be the last word." And immediately one thinks of the Ukranian president Volodymr Zelensky's words to Putin that Ukraine will have redress. Napayeva is offering a seemingly impossible simple solution: only allow people to just 'be' in their own place and there will be no need to impose belief, image, language or politics.

Solar Eclipse 1914 takes us to Arkseny Tarkovsky who was born in Yelisavetgrad (formerly the Soviet Union but now Kropvnytskyi, central Ukraine). For film buffs, a delightful way into poetry is via his celebrated son Andrei Tarkovsky's film *Mirror* which includes some voice-over of his father reading his own poems, allowing Russian and non-Russian speakers alike to capture what Peter France in the blurb describes as their "dream-like potency of suggestion".

In spite of the horrors of war, Tarkovsky maintains a degree of optimism in his poetry. This is due to a sustained, metaphysical stance in the Russian tradition of Tolstoyan pantheism, with the individual and nature part of a timeless continuum: "a world of secret correspondences" ('In the Woodman's Hut') and time as transcendent. As part of the generation influenced by Silver Age poets one can hear half-echoes of Boris Pasternak's 'When the Weather Clears Up' in Tarkovksy's lines that read also as manifesto:

> How I would like to breathe into my verses
> this whole world with its constant restlessness,
> the tiny movement of the meadow grasses,
>
> the grandeur, vague but instantaneous,
> of trees, or birds that rise into the sky,
> like swirls of sand in twittering nervousness –   ('Rain')

His awe at the world starts out with life-affirming nature poems, where he looks as through a magnifying glass at seemingly insignificant details: "I...dare not displace / this miniature pharaoh's / resting-place" ('Moth'). And even when merging it with the war context he maintains this sense of wonder: "... I fashioned / these birds with my very own hands / like the dead gripping day in the trenches / while we, with our bayonet gashes, / slept on in the trenches till day." ('Pigeons in the Square').

The collection's crowning pinnacle is the superb title poem which recalls the total eclipse of the sun that took place at the start of World War One just as Russian was invading East Prussia. Tarkovsky takes this childhood memory of receiving the gift of a rifle shell by a deserter – itself an interesting merging of kindness and war – at such an apocalyptic moment to combine collective mourning "In the summer a nation in mourning / was bound in iron chains" with a message of life's survival from the natural world. Note, in particular, Tarkovsky's clever combining of the glimmer of light from the disappearing sun with a very concrete image of a Russian scythe:

> And as if through the eyes of an icon
> he watched as the diamond light
> of the brilliant sickle low in the skies
> narrowed then vanished from sight.

And recalling that motionless moment
from a world unlike any before,
I understood that alien stamp
in eyes that are scorched by war.

And darkness fell. He departed.
And as a kind of farewell
in the silence, deep and green as sleep,
he left me a rifle shell.

And suddenly – that brilliant light...
I'd fathomed it to the core...

How long I've lived! A hundred years!...
    ...A thousand years or more!   ('Solar Eclipse 1914')

Somehow all converges to indicate life, no matter what continues.

In the later poems, Tarkovsky's affirmative mindset cannot free him from many of war's darker themes: lost love, "She'll hold out a hand that bears no ring of mine" ('Roses in Crystal'); survivor guilt "Whom can I tell which way the wind is blowing, / how green the grass is or how blue the sky?" ('In Memory of Friends'); and the, now particularly relevant, fate of refugees, "The icy wind bites at my feet. Yet, I / am just a refugee, no use at all / to anyone! You don't care if I die!" ('Refugee')

Yet, like Napeyeva, Tarkovsky still holds on to faith in the word to transcend individual tragedy as it "holds the power of centuries":

for though each word is just a shell,
is just a skin, it stores
your destiny – waits, hones its blades
in every line of yours.   ('Words')

BELINDA COOKE

PREGNANT IRISH BULLS FROM YORKSHIRE

New and Selected Poems by Ian Duhig. Picador Poets. 112pp.; £14.99.

Ian Duhig's verse is the product of an immensely fertile and active mind, a mind seeded, as it were, by multifarious sources – scholarly and popular, medieval and modern, English and Irish, to name but a few. The jumping-off points for individual poems are as likely to be provided by a Roman curse-tablet found in Bath ('Vilbia') as by the Ribblehead Viaduct (part 5 in 'Jericho Shanty'); by Federico Garcia Lorca ('A Lorca Gacela') or by Amy Johnson ('The Last Testament of Amy Johnson') or Georges Braque ('Braque's Drum'). The range of Duhig's omnivorous reading is reflected in the presence of epigraphs from, *inter alia*, Jorie Graham ('Irish Fever'), Catherine Cookson ('Glass Talk'), Geoffrey of Monmouth ('Indirections') and Dickens ('Behoof') – all of the examples cited here are to be found in this *New and Selected Poems*.

If I remember rightly, the first collection by Ian Duhig which I read was *The Mersey Goldfish* (1995). I won't pretend that I immediately became an admirer of Duhig's work, though I certainly found it striking; I enjoyed especially the wit in which Duhig used his often out-of-the-way erudition, for example, 'Gloss', a poem reprinted here. Looking back through my notebook of the time, I find that I tentatively pigeonholed Duhig as an heir to that 'tradition of learned wit' on which the scholar D. W. Jefferson had published an influential essay some years before, '*Tristram Shandy* and the Tradition of Learned Wit' (*Essays in Criticism*, 1(3), 1951, pp.222-248). Jefferson traces this tradition (a review such as this is not the place to summarise quite what he has to say about it) through such figures as Rabelais, Erasmus, Cervantes, Robert Burton, Sir Thomas Browne and Jonathan Swift. For Jefferson's purposes, the tradition effectively ends with Sterne, but a case could easily be made that writers such as Joyce, Nabokov, Flann O'Brien, Borges and Orhan Pamuk have continued it. When I had read more of Duhig, I began to suspect that he had a lot in common with Sterne in particular. That suspicion was confirmed with the publication of *Digressions* (Smokestack Books, 2014). This was a collaborative book, created by Duhig and the artist Philippa Troutman on the occasion, in 2013, of the tercentenary of Sterne's birth.

There are clear intellectual and literary affinities between Sterne and Duhig. Each has made statements about his writing which the other would, I feel sure, endorse. The online page devoted to Ian Duhig at the Poetry Archive (poetryarchive.org) quotes him as saying "I do mock literature and take it seriously at the same time" – which identifies precisely the duality which sustains *Tristram Shandy* (though Sterne might have replaced the word "literature" by "the novel". Or, to reverse the roles as it were, what Sterne declares in the opening paragraph of Chapter XI of Volume II of *Tristram Shandy* is entirely apt with regard to Duhig's poetry: "Writing when properly managed … is but a different name for conversation: As no one, who knows what he is about in good company, would venture to talk all; – so no author … would presume to think all: The truest respect you can pay to the reader's understanding is to halve this matter amicably, and leave him something to imagine in turn, as well as yourself." While none of Duhig's poems are wilfully hermetic, more than a few of them do require an active reader, a reader willing and able "to imagine in turn". Sterne and Duhig also share a fondness for digressions. Sterne (*Tristram Shandy*, I.xxii) declares "Digressions, incontestably, are the sunshine; – they are the life, the soul of reading", sentiments of which, I suspect, Duhig would approve. There are biographical comparisons to be drawn too. Both writers have an Irish background. Sterne's father was English, but the writer was born in Ireland. Duhig points out in his 'Afterforeword' (!) to *Digressions* (p.60) that "Tipperary [was] where Sterne (and my father) were born". Both Duhig and Sterne became, and flourished as, writers in Yorkshire; Sterne – whose great-grandfather Richard Sterne (c.1596-1683) was archbishop of York – was born in Clonmel, Tipperary and lived there until the age of ten, when he was sent to live in Yorkshire with an uncle and attend school there; when aged 20 he began studies at Jesus College, Cambridge and subsequently entered the church. In 1738 he became vicar of Sutton-on-the-Forest, 8 miles north of York. From 1760 to 1768 he was perpetual curate of Coxwold, also north of York, living in a house now known as Shandy Hall. The nine volumes of *Tristram Shandy* were published between 1759 and 1767. Ian Duhig's parents emigrated to England in the 1950s and Duhig was born in London (in 1954), the eighth of eleven children; the family lived among the London-Irish community, centred on Paddington and Kilburn. Duhig left school after his O-levels and moved to Leeds – another city with a well-established Irish community. Duhig went on to study at Leeds University and has been based in the city since then.

Both Duhig and Sterne are fascinated by the non-verbal, 'material', resources available to the writer. Sterne famously included marbled pages and the like in *Tristram Shandy*. In Volume I a double-sided black page is inserted between Chapters XII and XIII, to mark the death of Yorick. In Volume VI a blank page appears (as part of Chapter

XXXVIII) on which the reader is invited to create his own image of female beauty, "paint her to your own mind – as like your mistress as you can – as unlike your wife as your conscience will let you", rather than making do with Sterne's own description of Widow Wadman, the lady 'loved' by Uncle Toby. Although Duhig doesn't require his publisher to incorporate within his text the marbled, black or blank pages used by Sterne, he does structure poems in terms of the materiality of a text and refer to such features. A good example is provided by 'Margin Prayer from an Ancient Psalter' (New and Selected Poems, 30-31), which takes the form of a dramatic monologue by a bored scribe in an Irish monastery who is obliged to copy *The Grey Psalter of Antrim*, which interests him not at all. We are to imagine that he has written his complaints in the margin: "It has the magic realism of an argumentum: / it has the narrative subtlety of the Calendar of Oengus; / … it grips like the Colophon to the Book of Durrow / it deconstructs like a canon-table; / it makes St. Jerome's Defence of his Vulgate look racy. / I would make a gift of it to Halfdane the Sacker / that he might use it to wipe his wide Danish arse." The poem is split into two sections, the gap between the two carrying this note: "(Text illegible here because of teeth marks)". After the poem's last line this statement appears – "(Text completely illegible from this point / Because of lake water and otter dung)". This is a device also used elsewhere in the 'tradition of learned wit' as, for example, when Rabelais in Book I, Chapter 1 of *La vie de Gargantua et de Pantagruel* tells his reader that he will be presenting as much as he can of an ancient book of which "the rats and moths, or (that I may not lie) other wicked beasts, had nibbled off the beginning". (My quotation is taken from the seventeenth-century translation by Sir Thomas Urquhart).

In *Nominies* (Bloodaxe, 1998, p.4), but not included in this new volume, is the four line 'True Vision of the Virgin', appearing at the top of an otherwise blank page:

> For his climactic Divine comic strip
> Illustrating Dante's Paradiso
> Botticelli wrote this title, then stopped
> And left the vellum blank. It was as though …

Sterne's blank page has taken on a sacred dimension.

In 'Calculating Chance' (*Digressions*, 16-17) Duhig finds after, he tells us, trying to use his copy of Sterne for a kind of "*Sortes Shandeana*" – a personal variation on the Sortes Vergilianae – that "the calfskin grows into an Irish bull". An 'Irish bull' (besides being a type of livestock) is/was a self-contradictory statement, which might be made consciously or unconsciously. One example might be what Gwendolen says to Jack Worthing in *The Importance of Being Earnest*, "If you are not too long, I will wait for you here all my life". Duhig's poem has an epigraph: "An Irish bull is always pregnant" *John Pentland Mahaffy*. J.P. Mahaffy (1839-1919) was a Dublin classicist and famous wit who became, in the last years of his life, Provost of Trinity College Dublin. Vivian Mercier, in his classic book *The Irish Comic Tradition* (Oxford, 1953, p. 112) writes "It was Mahaffy who supplied the perfect definition of an Irish bull, 'A male animal that is always pregnant". As well as being a 'perfect definition', Mahaffy's words are themselves a 'perfect' Irish bull. Poets and mystics have, of course, long known that self-contradictory statements can be 'pregnant' with meaning. Examples abound; a couple must suffice. First, from the Book IV of the *White Yajurveda*, translated by Ralph T.H. Griffith (1899):

> It, standing still, outstrips the others running…
> It moveth; it is motionless. It is far distant; it is near.
> It is within This All; and it surrounds This All externally.

Second, from Shakespeare's 'The Phoenix and Turtle':

> Reason, in itself confounded,
> Saw division grow together,
> To themselves yet either neither,
> Simple were so well compounded,
>
> That it cried, How true a twain
> Seemeth this concordant one!

In recent decades, some philosophers have taken the view that self-contradictory statements can be meaningful. See, for example, the entry 'Dialetheism' in the online Stanford Encyclopaedia of Philosophy (https://plato.stanford.edu/entries/dialetheism/). Duhig has produced at least one splendid Irish bull – the brief poem 'De Senectute' (*The Speed of Dark*, Picador, 2007, p.41). It reads, in full:

> although I am now senile
> at least I'm not senile

While Ian Duhig's work may not abound in 'simple' Irish bulls (can an Irish bull ever be simple?), I think its spirit permeates his work (as it permeates Sterne's). Much of Duhig's poetry is full of related devices such as wordplay, paradox, double meanings and ambiguities. Although Duhig's voice can be, as occasion requires, angry or compassionate, there is an overriding sense of joyous delight in the plasticity of language, in its fertile instability. Anyone not familiar with Duhig's work should try to take the opportunity offered by this volume of *New and Selected Poems*.

The rules of the Association of Book Reviewers require that any member reviewing a volume containing the word 'Selected' in its title should complain about omissions. I will finish, therefore, by saying, that this book would have been better for the presence of poems such as 'Portrait of the Art' (from *The Mersey Goldfish*), 'Use Complete Sentences' and 'Fauvel's Fountain' (*The Speed of Dark*), 'A Line from Snorri Sturluson' (*Nominies*) and 'Taking my Measure' (*The Lammas Hireling*)', before exercising my own right to self-contradiction by saying also that I love the book as it is!

GLYN PURSGLOVE

ABSENCE AND LONGING, RESILIENCE AND SURVIVAL
Swimming to Albania by Sue Hubbard. Salmon Poetry. 78 pp.; £12
Siege and Symphony by Myra Schneider. Second Light Publications. 86 pp.; £9.95

In 'Those Far Blue Hills', Sue Hubbard self-identifies as "a storyteller / of absence and loss". Appropriate then, to start with an image of what is largely absent from her poems. In 'Barreiro', a rundown town in Portugal is described: its people, graffiti, "opera-set houses" and "wrecked staircases". But what stands out is a young mother whose t-shirt brags in English: "I'm exactly where I need to be". Of all the possible things to notice, this impacts this poet because her writing contrasts such assurance and existential confidence: Hubbard's focus is on absence, not presence, longing, not fulfilment, what-might-have-been rather than what is (though what is, is often vividly and eloquently portrayed). There is a clear line to be drawn to this new work from

Hubbard's second collection, *Ghost Station* (Salt, 2004), with its epigraph from Fernando Pessoa: "Some have a great dream in life and fall short of it".

Growing up in the stifling 1950s, Hubbard's poems of childhood are full of enjoyable period details. Two sisters, in a London park, are dressed in "camel coats / with beaver collars" ('1955, perhaps?'). A mother, in a photograph, wears "summer shorts" and sports her "Hedy Lamarr hair" ('June'). A girl "dunk[s] net petticoats into sugar solution // to froth out the nylon frills / of [her] first dance dress" ('Snow'). But possessions, beloved of the middle classes, "cannot take me in their arms" ('Inheritance') and family relationships, particularly with the young girl's father, are summed up in the collection of hats left hanging in the tallboy after his death: "there's silence everywhere" ('Hats'). Such an absence of contact and fulfilment seems to spill over into later life, throughout which – and this is the sort of naked declaration Hubbard excels at – the one thing that has always mattered is "to wake / mirrored in another's gaze: / its unplumbed depths" ('one thing'). The directness and (even) ferocity of such a statement convinces, though in the aftermath one might want to scrutinise the assumptions, ironies, even the language of it.

An untypical dramatic monologue, 'Earth-Dreams', voices a mermaid's yearning for life on land and the love of a human: "Over and over I've tried to imagine // a need for balance, that slow steadying of the inner ear, / metatarsals pushing into solid ground". She pictures the absent love object, but wakes each morning only to water, where "there is only silence". Taking up the watery imagery, the lonely narrator of 'Lake' finds its allure too powerful. Despite the business (above all the business of the poet, a business Hubbard pursues so well) of "being / in this moment and this   following every / tilt and shift of the world", the temptation to immerse herself is irresistible. Ironically providing stunning details of her descent, she dives, suicidally, "till I can no longer go on holding my breath".

Perhaps travel promises escape from the self's perceived failings, felt absence and self-consciousness? The final section of *Swimming to Albania* is rich in touristic details of southern Europe, but Hubbard knows "all travel / is a form of return" ('Those Far Blue Hills') and even in Italy, the evening walk must be taken "in arm with what might have been" ('Lost'). Pessoa and the city of Lisbon still remain touchstones for Hubbard. In 'Remembering Pessoa', she imagines adopting the Portuguese poet's mode of life (attracted perhaps to his continual re-invention of himself in his proliferating heteronyms). The modal verbs of imagined possibility structure this poem – the disengaged life of the *flâneuse*, the temptations of love – but in the end: "My head aches because / my heart aches, so I write / and write to give meaning / to what isn't there."

Hubbard's work has a relatively narrow range, her palette of forms and tones likewise. But we do not (if we have any sense) want Wordsworth to show more knowledge of the streets, ask Larkin to cheer up a bit, insist Lowell should stop talking about himself. There is a type of art that confidently positions itself early and continues to work that seam.

In Myra Schneider's poem 'Trees', the narrator also suffers an "ache in my head", but, significantly, she finds definitive relief in the natural world (albeit a north London park): "it's as if / I'm in the heart of an ancient wood in a distant place". Schneider's narrators contrast Hubbard's in that they know exactly where they need to be. There is a recurring trope of the retreat to nature. In 'Cushion Moss', the "sad paragraphs" in a newspaper present the "ache" and pain of the world; the local park again offers up a natural detail – the vivid green of moss – as a balm in the first place ("a green which fills my mind, feeds my arteries") and, as so often in Schneider's work, secondly as instruction or inspiration: "a green that urges: never give up". The imperatives of the natural world (as read by this poet) are often ventriloquised by her. "Listen to green and fling open your windows", declares 'Inside Green' and then urgently, "don't linger . . Marvel . . love it . . Be still".

Such faith means *Siege and Symphony* has plenty of poems concerned with environmental degradation. There is a frequent anger at the "racket" and "plastic" of human creation, but the book's opening poem is more characteristic. A sycamore in the beloved local park has been condemned and is felled to no more than a "table-top". Then someone sets it alight. The poet goes out, expecting to be attending a death, but:

> To my surprise it's only charred
> and the spines
>   are now a crown of spindly branches notched
>   with buds, sturdy promises of green leaf.

The poem is titled 'Resurgence' and might have been called 'natural resilience'. However, Schneider's frequent desire to point her moral means the above lines are followed by these: "I'm so moved by the resolve to live in this world / my heart rises to the sky as if it's a songbird". Such a 'palpable design' on the reader (as Keats called it) feels manipulative, though the poet's spirit and intent are unimpeachable. Schneider wears her heart on her sleeve. Church-visiting in Cropthorne, in the Vale of Evesham, she wonders why she does it, not being "a Christian". Her faith is the same as Wordsworth's as he viewed Tintern Abbey: in a force which "rolls through all things", natural and human, which Schneider summarises as a kind of life force, as "the will to survive". It is largely this faith which allows her writing to escape the prisons of self-consciousness, of individual sadness, of the effects of old age, to empathise with others. 'Lake Orta' opens with such a feeling for those who have been displaced:

> If you've wrenched yourself from the swaddle of first language
> and the home which has always kept you, your feelings safe,
> because, exposed to gunfire, it couldn't mother you any longer [. . .]

The proffered salve remains the same – a recourse to nature, this time in the Italian lakes. The water, mountains, birds and ferryman perhaps trip a little too easily into the poem, but also, perhaps, ask here to be read more emblematically.

Her belief in the resilience of the human spirit and its expression through art makes it obvious why Schneider was drawn to the material which makes up the long, eponymous poem which concludes this, her sixteenth collection. This sequence of poems leans several narratives together: that of Shostakovich's composition of his seventh symphony, the 'Leningrad'; the experiences of people during the siege of Leningrad, 1941 to 1944; and moments from the poet's own life. But for this reader, the paralleling of events does not really spark, nor does the evident empathy sufficiently rise clear of the details of historical research. Schneider's more natural mode finds her remembering a homeless boy in central London. The gulf between the wealthy environment, the diners in restaurants, and the plight of this "slip of a boy" is poignantly explored. But Schneider moves beyond observation when the narrator encounters the boy again and "I buy him a sandwich in Tesco". This moment, when the poet sets aside her notebook and puts her hand into her pocket to offer help, is startling as if breaking the fourth wall of the poem in expectation of corresponding actions from the reader. In *Siege and Symphony,* there is not just artistic achievement, an urgent desire to communicate, writing which celebrates life in its many forms, but also a powerful example and moral imperative.

MARTYN CRUCEFIX

WHISPERS INSIDE THE HOUR-GLASS
Liffey Sequence by David Butler. Doire Press. 95pp.; €13

Liffey Sequence is David Butler's third full-length collection of poems. It contains two sequences of poems about specific places. The 'Blackrock Sequence' was commissioned by Dun Laoghaire-Rathdown County Council and originally published in a limited edition, with illustrations by David's brother Jim, and won the World Illustration Awards in 2018; it focuses on the landmarks of this area on the outskirts of Dublin. The collection is concluded by 'Liffey Sequence' which focuses on Dublin itself. These two sets of poems top and tail the collection and between them is a wide ranging selection of poems on diverse themes, including topics such as meditations on ageing and death, the White Rose German resistance movement, Bleriot's flying machine, the gold boat from the Broighter hoard, the macabre display of semi-mummified corpses in the Capuchin Catacombs of Palermo, with poems in Gaelic and one in Portuguese (by Fernando Pessoa) in the original and English translations; there are also ekphrastic poems inspired by paintings and music (Vermeer, van Gogh, Debussy). There is a strong awareness of mortality running through many of the poems, highlighting the transitory nature of things and the fragility of life. The 'Blackrock Sequence' opens by giving us a stunning 'aerial' view of the coast:

> See it again as memory soars
> over towers driven like rivets
> to hold down the hem of the bay;
> over bandstand and pagoda,
> terraces, cloistered squares, to where
> harbour mandibles enfold
> the skittishness of metronomes.

The rest of the sequence provides meditations on the various well-known sites, such as the forty foot bathing place ("at the end of the jetty, / in the howling wind, one equinox / never to be forgotten") which is a reference to a transformative event recalled in Samuel Beckett's play *Krapp's Last Tape*. Then there's the Martello tower ("sentinels in a time of revolution") where James Joyce lived for a time ("from platform for ordnance to artists' squat"). Butler neatly conjures up the relics of colonialism in the British monarchs' initials on old post-boxes: "Edwardian terraces; the Royal St George, / the pillar-boxes, VR, ER, GR; post-colonial." The present and the past merge in these delicate evocations of Blackrock where: "Memory persists, / stubborn as a crustacean / in the seawall's flank".

'Liffey Sequence', which concludes the book, is a rather ironic love poem to the city of Dublin, with the "roasting tang / the old olfactory memory / the nut waft of bitter hops / over the vats of James's Gate" which is the location of the famous Guinness brewery. We follow the river Liffey through the city, starting in 'Wake' by crossing the Heuston Bridge in a tram: "Wake to the clang and clamour – / the cowbell and slow glissando / of a tram as its heft glides across / Heuston Bridge, townward." Later we pass the war memorial: "That shambles was never our war. / Yet they fought, too, our great-uncles, / and came back to a fractured land." And the Famine Memorial statues where: "were the dead to rise / they'd weigh no more / than a shadow weighs / passing / over the dry-stone of the land". The elegance of the Samuel Beckett bridge, designed by Calatrava to look like a harp, is celebrated: "the thirty-something cable-stays arranged / by diminished octave, left to right, / as if awaiting only the touch / of an Aeolian harper."

But the beauty is balanced by the presence of poverty, both in the past in 'Dockers, 1930' who "scrimmage about / the rough pulpit to catch 'the read', the foreman / meting out who works, who idles." And the present day homeless, begging on the street:

> On how many bridges, a squat –
> cardboard sign and polystyrene
> to catch a casual charity,
> the weather-cudgelled faces
> lit by a gaudy sunset?

In these poems Dublin is portrayed in all its particularity but it is also universally representative of any capital city with its contrasts of elegance and displays of confidence alongside scars of the past and present problems.

In contrast to the tightly focussed sequences that bookend the collection the central portion of the book is full of diversity. There are vivid sights, for instance in 'Light Rail' where: "the first slow train unspooling / its show-reel across a bridge / in a series of stills, the sitters / sleep-stunned and solitary / as anything from Hopper". In the Musée des Arts et Métiers Blériot's plane: "...hangs like a fallen angel's remains / from the vault of a deconsecrated priory, / startling as a Duchamp ready-made". In 'Leaf Storm':

> a puckish wind stirred up and,
> like Dante's fugitives, drove all
> about a streaming leaf storm,
> shoal-dense and endless, brass
> upon brass, chattering, sheering

As the quotations show, Butler has a painter's eye for conjuring up striking visual images. Throughout the collection there is a deeply moving evocation of the permeability of the past and present and the elusive quest for fulfilment. A stand-out poem is 'These Are Not Days', a meditation on the fleetingness of time and the insubstantiality of all our endeavours:

> Count them up, and they come to years,
> but years empty of substance.
> They are the dry husks of our lives,
> the whisper inside the hour-glass.
>
> Days are not the coinage of will,
> as once we imagined.
> One day they rise like locusts,
> to devour us.

Liffey Sequence is an excellent collection which provides a powerful portrait in poetry of Dublin and of so much else as well.

COLIN PINK

SPECIFICITIES

Brooksong & Shadows by Lynne Wycherley. Shoestring Press. 58pp.; £9.

Lynne Wycherley's new collection, her sixth, falls into two parts, Brooksong and Shadows, Otterton and the Great War – a sequence of seventeen numbered and titled poems concluding with a Coda – and Path of the Dancing Hare, Otterton and beyond (2021), a group of poems that circles around the same Devon landscape with the focus more on present times and contemporary people. Formally, the poems across the collection share the same characteristics: a predominance of short lines and short stanza forms, lyric rhythms and shaping, and compressed and concentrated modes of expression that frequently create a jewel-like precision of effect.

The sequence about Otterton and the First World War remembers specific individuals from this community who died in the war by name, aligning them with observations of the natural scene in a way that suggests the redemptive, healing power of their local landscapes and the natural world:

> as if the cobalt wears them,
> rain-beads on its sleeve
>
> Frank White, Gilbert Follett,
> Goldney Hart, John Gorman
>
> as if the grass will bear them,
> tourmalines in its weave   ('Tree of Remembrance')

The women of the community, and their lace-making, are present, too ("'Streamside', Aunt Martha Smith,/ Honiton work in her time-knurled hands", 'Bobbins in the Lee') while the various purposeful traditional crafts these women and men were skilled in (and implicitly, perhaps, the craft of poetry) stand in pointed contrast to the senseless destructiveness of war. The same compressed mode – very specific vocabulary and detail, forged into a lyric shape – is used to evoke violent war experiences to striking effect:

> Barrage!
> Shatter-black, flung jets.
> Vent! Vent! Volcanic.
> The night is epileptic.   ('The Fire-step')

'Diamond-Cut Doors, St Michael's' – one of several poems in the second part of the book with dedications to specific, presumably local individuals – describes the engraved glass doors in Otterton's church, but also seems to me to capture something of the quality of the poetry thoughout: "so fine you can almost hear/the diamond-point drill". There's a kind of poetic precision-tooling going on here, and I was interested in the way this sometimes created effects verging on the abstract, as much about sonic and linguistic patterning as visual description:

> How heifers,
> contoured, cave-paint
> the dusk, a Hereford's rust,
> barn owls icing
> the baize –
>
> Cressets in time.
> This ingle: their shine.
> Pennons! Blazons!
> Un-erased.   ('As Cattle Fade to Curlews')

Beyond the dedicated focus of this "diamond-point drill", beyond the dedications to individuals, there is a strong sense of the poet's own mission sustaining the impulse behind the poetry throughout. The Prologue poem which opens the collection, 'She Returns to the Farm', introduces the poems that follow as a kind of healing enterprise ("No need to speak; her bones/ mentor me. I breathe; mend; begin."), while 'Pilgrimage', which opens the second part of the book, reaffirms the restorative power of the natural world, this time in contrast not with war but with the distractions and depletions of modern life – in the country lane there are

> No pixels but pollen,
> no touch-screen but sky,
> no kerb to weave a city,
> warring greys.

'Hare on the Headland' captures the guiding spirit of the poet's approach, emulating the hare which she hopes will escape traps and dangers and leap away: "Light-footed sister / I'll live in your lee,/ faithful to fields, mercurial, free."

Reading these poems in my own semi-urban location, looking up words as I went along online (my vocabulary has been considerably enriched by the experience), I felt sometimes that these finely-crafted poems were operating in a sphere which although often beautiful was somehow beyond my reach. Some descriptions – a river's "dancing silvers", "sun-trembled rain", wind's "wild opals" – I felt were signalling the poet's own delight in these scenes rather than allowing the reader, too, to be present. (Or just this reader, perhaps: this may well be a question of personal taste and different for others.) But I did admire the craft, cohesion and linguistic adventurousness of a collection that is all of a piece, entirely consistent with itself, in both its overall structure and its individual forms, resonant with specificity.

SUSAN MACKERVOY

DREAMING DIFFERENTLY
Spoil by Morag Smith. Broken Sleep Books. 36pp.; £6.50
Dreamlines by Jenny Johnson. Emoter's Gap, Eskdale Publishing. 112pp.; £12
Lyonesse by Penelope Shuttle. Bloodaxe. 152pp.; £12.99

Penelope Shuttle has had a very public career as a writer and poet and Jenny Johnson has been an altogether more private figure, but I always think of them as contemporaries with a great deal in common. Both were born in the mid Forties and have had long careers stretching from the Seventies right up to the present. Both had a decidedly surreal energy at the beginning. Shuttle was frequently both obscure and adventurous in the Seventies writing poetic prose that interested Ted Hughes among others. However, she became arguably less so as she became Peter Redgrove's partner, the joint author of *The Wise Wound* and an established poet, published by Oxford University Press with perhaps a movement towards verbal abstraction. Johnson had a strong human presence lurking in her fine, rather abstract early sequences *Becoming* and *A Year of Dreams* (which was awarded a South West Arts prize by Ted Hughes). Dream and image and myth interact, but Johnson's early work is also one of the few places among the poetry of circa 1980 that you meet original rhythms and sounds. Then her poems became much more obviously about people and less obviously musical, though no less on the edge of dream, as her work moved into the

Nineties. A gap of some years followed while she wrote dances rather than poems, but then Johnson composed the poems in *Dreamlines*, the volume under review, which are very different to what came before, for the poems are longer and more intricate and with a very different music. Shuttle wrote some of her most important work in the interval that Johnson was silent, especially the fine and very direct elegies for Peter Redgrove, but also the lively, more playful, though perhaps slighter poems of *Will You Walk A Little Faster?* But like Johnson's *Dreamlines,* Shuttle's new book *Lyonesse* is genuinely a new departure.

But before I get into these two large volumes I want to talk about Morag Smith's fine short collection *Spoil,* which loses nothing in comparison. A mere twenty poems, but they are very fine. I sometimes wonder if the old idea prior to the mid Seventies of books of forty-eight and no more than sixty-four pages, and pamphlets of around twenty pages, did not have a lot to be said for it. At least the poems had to be sifted to the best ones, which cut out the dross. Anyway I don't think there is a superfluous poem in *Spoil.* The music is sonorous, yet astringent and perhaps closer to Johnson in her earlier days than Shuttle, but also totally different. Lines are the only punctuation, which is often the downfall of would-be modern poets, but here it is handled immaculately:

> Spoil
> rising gently to the lip
> once heaped up
> now falls stone by stone
> into the dark beneath...   ('Great Flat Lode')

The poems fall into two categories. There are the ones that relate to Cornwall's soil and mining history and poverty and hence obviously the title. However, equally there are very tough, good poems about being on the road with small children in tow: "We drive from farm to farm / awaiting a harvest / that never comes / diesel diminishing / Everywhere's the same / *not-yet* / *not-yet*.... / beg the shop to tick me / a packet of nappies / some bread / a few vegetables" ('Elvis the Enforcer'). And similarly 'Rabbits, Eye on the Mirror' and several others. What makes these work for me is their quality of coming out of the imagination and the mind in an almost dream-like way; they ought to be merely realistic, but somehow are not. Possibly the author's Zen

Buddhism plays a part, but equally likely it is the constant interactions of sounds. And this sense of a dream of reality is even more so in the Cornish poems. Yes, the mines and geology of Cornwall and the mistreatment of women in the old mines all play a part, but what makes these poems is the sense of one living earth, of which all these elements are part: "Behind me / the hill rises up / but under me / the ground is broken // Grubbed in the dark / holder of seeds / turn shit black / I am the fifty foot woman / up to my neck in it" ('Salt of the Earth').

Anyway suffice it to say that this is the liveliest collection by a poet I have not come across before in quite a while.

Jenny Johnson's *Dreamlines* is much more obviously dreamy than *Spoil*. Indeed except perhaps for the *Octet* section at the end of the book the poems are based on the poet's dreams. Yet, whereas with Morag Smith you stop and notice the dreaminess that surrounds the stark realities, with Johnson you have to pause and think about the very strong sense of the real world that is inherent in her dreaminess. Sometimes indeed it is difficult to separate dream from reality. Thus from 'The Promise':

> ...a telephone rings. The police
> have found my son on the ground, unconscious –
>
> have assumed that his malaise comes from an alcoholic binge.
> Veronica intervenes. "Does his breath smell of almonds?"
> I think of cyanide within its ridged bottle.
>
> When we are told that Gawm has been taken to hospital –
> the nineteen thirties one, with its imitation Dutch gables –
> we drive there immediately, uncertain which entrance to approach.

However, this is not somehow quite real, which is perhaps indicated by the poem's opening lines:

> The November tides have toyed for hours
> with Gawm, Veronica and me ...

And similarly the sound patterns build the atmosphere of a parallel world to the real one, despite the apparent prosiness. Note the play on the d's of *almond, cyanide* and *ridged* in the second stanza above, or the uneasy clash of *bottle, hospital* and *gables*. Indeed Johnson playfully tells us about herself in the third person, 'her poems are appreciated most when read aloud.' and one can see why. There again the long lines, which at first sight seem prosy, have a way of taking you with them into the poems' own reality and revealing their music.

It is a strange world that Johnson leads us through. Various names, Gladys, Leighton, Felix and others recur doing almost real things, but often much odder. Whenever Gawm appears as in the passage above, I notice my own ears prick up and we get closer to reality. A fair number of the dreams apparently arise from an unhappy academic experience, a problem which a lot of poets from Wordsworth down have shared. And there seem to be memories of music lessons a long time ago. Occasionally, perhaps inevitably in a book with so many poems, I do feel we are on automatic pilot, or one bit of a poem simply does not go with another one. 'Anaemia' for example starts splendidly:

> I confine my poems to a listed building –
> scribble them in brick-powder on the top storey.

I could imagine a very fine poem developing from that. However it then drifts all over the place and we find among other things:

> The Leech family gapes at us from their side seats
> as the infant is lowered onto a bench and sedated.

And the Leech family I have to say annoys me. This is the disadvantage of the method; dreams are not all equally interesting and sometimes fragmented; and maybe the book would have been better a bit shorter. However, let us not get too carried away with criticism. The standard is very high and the book is very readable and enhanced by Anthony Wooten's colour illustrations. I think my own favourite poem is from the *Octet* section. 'On the Other Side' is seemingly a rather beautiful poem about the approach of age, though as always with Johnson it is slightly indefinite:

> Later on, turning round in a homeward field – turning west –
> you notice those roses, those vermilion heads above the hedgerow.

> From the other side of the railway track, they are calling you back …
> You are warned.

> "Not now," you repeat, "Not now."

With Penelope Shuttle's *Lyonesse* we are somewhere between *Spoil* and *Dreamlines*. The book is partly at least the result of long residence in Cornwall and collision with its history and myths. Lyonesse is the ancient, probably mythical kingdom that supposedly disappeared beneath the sea somewhere in the vicinity of Devon and Cornwall. However, the sequence according to Shuttle's lively and informative Preface owes much to a collision with an exhibition about the now sunken cities of the ancient world. She quotes too from Adrienne Rich's fine poem 'Diving into the Wreck', which I have always read as Rich's discovery of her own sexuality, but Shuttle says of herself and *Lyonesse* that it became a new way to write about loss, to explore "the allure of the past, the vanities of the present, the perils of the future. I sought to hold on to the sense that 'nothing is ever truly lost.'" In short, diving into *Lyonesse* gave her a new psychic reality and the opening poem of the sequence 'Door' says simply:

> I opened a door   found myself a city under the sea
> where everyone knew me by name…
> breathing salt water instead of air …

The good thing about *Lyonesse* is the genuine sense of compulsion. The weakness (if it is a weakness) is the tendency to leap in every possible direction the theme can give rise to and the directions are sometimes very slight. And yet there are some very fine poems, as good as any currently being written. 'Legends' for example:

> The lions of Lyonesse
> were legends
> in their own raw lunchtime…
>
> The *lewyon* of Lionville
> knew their place
> no one   and nothing above them
>
> those golden guys with manes
> and gaping slavering jaws
> the piss-backward lords of Lyonesse

Or there is 'Interviewing Neptune', which has a touch in common with Neptune's Greek namesake Okeoanos' pompous speech in *Prometheus Bound,* and is not a bad parody of some contemporary TV interviews and the refusal of politicians to comment: "Do you plan to retire, Oceanus, / to your own place in the sun? / And also, Majesty, / what is your opinion of rivers? // *No comment*" Or 'The Devil', which despite a certain playfulness turns strange at the end: "but it was the Devil's weather-work / conjuring up a ghost-city / from the last Glacial Maximum, / lost Loonois / gone again in an hour"

But these are all rather male quotes and a lot of the writing is very female, 'Sewing Lesson under the Sea' for example:

> Cut and piece a marriage quilt
> from your bloke's raised fist....
>
> Stretch the bruise-black fabric
> over the birch wood frame.
>
> Say your wishes, one, two, three.
> This quilt will be the making of you.

The endearing thing about *Lyonesse* is its sense of genuine inspiration. I am not sure every single poem should be there, for some as I say are very slight, but even the slight ones feel as if they jumped out at the poet. Certainly *Lyonesse* is well worth reading and has the freshness of a much younger poet.

Much the same can be said about the second half of the book, *New Lamps for Old*. This we are told was written at the same time as *Lyonesse* as a record of Shuttle's sadness after her husband's death turning to something more positive, and certainly there are some good elegiac poems. However there are also some very fine occasional poems and the sequence 'Ragged Stone Hill', which is full of the poet's love of the landscape, but also her sheer love of words:

> *Primacy* of daws is how it goes
> under Ragged Stone Hill
> despite the badger's quilly visits
> despite the here there gone of deer...

FRED BEAKE

POETRY COMMENT

With reviews of:

A Field Guide To Wedding Guests by Helen Reid. Poet's House Pamphlets. 28 pp.; £7.
Sleeping On The Wing by Eleanor Page. Against The Grain. 32 pp.; £6.
Bird Song And Nectar In The Silences by Lisa Lopresti. The Hedgehog Poetry Press. 22 pp.
Paper Doll by Katherine Lockton. Flipped Eye Publishing. 48 pp.
A Northumbrian Book Of Hours by Neil Curry. Wayleave Press. 20 pp.; £4.
Badlands by Hugo Williams. Mariscat Press. 32 pp.; £7.50.
The Giddings by John Greening. Mica Press. 36 pp.; £7.

In recent years it has been good, for both poet and reader, to see the resurgence of the pamphlet as a means of bringing poetry to the public. Roughly a quarter of the books Acumen receives for review are pamphlets. They are sometimes called chapbooks - small books "hawked by chapmen" (OED), or "chaps", rather inappropriate for offerings of poetry. I prefer pamphlet, a word derived from *pamphilet*, a popular form of the 12th century Latin *Pamphilus*, a love poem. Few modern pamphlets contain love poems, but they do deliver treats we would otherwise miss out on: first public utterances of fledgeling poets; sequences unencumbered by surrounding lesser poems; small helpings of work from established poets in between main courses. There are examples of each of these in the pamphlets I have chosen to comment on here.

Most of us would recognise at least some of the characters described in Helen Reid's debut pamphlet, *A Field Guide to Wedding Guests*. They range from the endearingly innocent 'Sullen Infanta' ("a tiny girl […] in the flurry of shuffling on the church steps"), through such dramatis personae as 'The Extra' ("who had been hurriedly ushered from the dance / [and] has re-emerged to loom tragically by the buffet") and 'The Great Aunt' ("on legs like / Twiglets in court shoes"), to the ravenous 'Distant Cousin' ("[wiping] lipstick off her canines") and the obnoxious 'Mr Tongue' ("someone's uncle in the disco dance, working the room"). The book's blurb tells us the poet "enjoys the absurd in the stuff of ordinary life". Reading Helen Reid puts me in mind of the conversations one has with one's other half when driving home from a function, remarking how awful certain guests were, gleefully elaborating on their worst points, then howling with laughter about them. Skilfully chosen, spot-on observations of the more absurd aspects of the human character can be curiously entertaining.

Interspersed between the nine wedding guest poems are nine other poems displaying a similar wit and precision, but rather more highly wrought, including three sonnets, a villanelle, a prose poem, and a delightful sequence of seven haikus entitled 'The Suburban Ornithologist'. Here is the haiku 'Outlands Road': "Pigeons are mating / on the TV aerial / during peak viewing." Helen Reid can tell a good story, setting the scene with well-chosen imagery. In the intriguing 'Press this Shell to your Ear', the tang of the sea heightens the allure of its brief narrative. The poem describes a relationship between "I" (a mermaid?) and "my silkie boy" (a seal-like creature). Driven south from "a northern winter shore": "All the way he kept up such a sea pup keening, / I had to toss a mermaid's purse for him to chew, / clamp a cowrie to his ear to make him sleep. / I dug a pond deep in my orchard where each pink dawn / he stripped down to his oily grey hide, / lay mournful in his landlocked pit of mud." The poem ends with the predictable separation: "I woke up in a sweet dry bed and found the cowrie / on his pillow, so that now and then, on a stormy night, / or a spring tide, I still can share his distant rushing joy."

I hope we see more of Helen Reid's entertaining poems.

Eleanor Page has something of the spirit of gentle John Clare. The poems in her debut pamphlet *Sleeping on the Wing* are much concerned with what is fragile or disappearing – fish from a pond, a metaphor for those being lost to Covid ('Nowhere to hide'), house moths ('Side by side'), stranded sea creatures ('Memories of You'), a cliff-top town ('Sea-malls, Dunwich'), fledglings amongst glass skyscrapers ('Light and so many small birds'), a Cabbage White butterfly ('Pieris rapae'). Her poems are remarkable for their empathy. In 'Memories of You', the poet finds herself at the scene of a mass stranding (dolphins?): "gripped by their eyes, coin-wide / and staring. I plead with them / to forgive me, but they just stare / and breathe and breathe and breathe. / I wait for the tide to drag them back; / there is so much I love there, I cannot / bring myself to bury them."

Page has a special interest in folklore and mythology. In the delicate three-part poem 'While You Were Sleeping', a response to Su Blackwell's 2004 art installation of the same name inspired by a Burmese legend, the soul of a young girl wanders as a butterfly while she sleeps: "You slept, pale as cotton // as I watched you through the night. // The firelight kept dying // from too much held breath. // Too many times I slipped awake // and can't tell if I dreamt // the white wings above your bed"

This is accomplished work. The poet is taking us to the edge of things, inhabiting mystery, climbing to the 'Krummholz' on the tree-line, writing home from the intersection between human and fellow-creature. The appearances of other humans in her poems are peripheral ('Whispers'), or no more than hinted at (who is the You in 'Memories of You'?), or distanced by time or tragedy as in 'Daisies (on never knowing you)': "They say you are out there somewhere / among the daisies, where you should have played. / I've searched, and though I have not found you / I spend so many moons amid their trembling". When she writes from places where humans throng, the poet concentrates on spirits ('Fern Frost') or the creatures that suffer there ('Light and so many small birds').

Eleanor Page is so much more than a nature poet and I encourage you to read her.

Lisa Lopresti's slim, attractively-produced pamphlet *Bird Song and Nectar in the Silences* contains just 13 poems, some of which sing as winsomely as I imagine the three budgerigars on the front cover sing. 'Take the Stars …' begins almost like a nursery rhyme: "Take the stars, in jars, / the sun in our butter, / moon beams through net curtains, / and sea sounds in sea shells. / Hold these close in memory". The poem is a lock-down poem, going on to describe the worry of inaction and separation, its last line "You can hear, the hack of magpies" a contrast in tone to "bird song and nectar in the silences", which for me is a fine choice for the title and the finest line in the pamphlet. It is the last line of the poem 'Rose Bombs', "*inspired by the Arabic musician Maya Youssef*", describing a recital, "this moment of notes", in which "She hopes that bombs turn into roses [...] High and low thrumming c[h]ords of danger, / sirocco dust blushing the blooms."

Lisa Lopresti is well-known on the Bristol poetry scene and her poems have been broadcast on BBC local radio. Her passion and creativity in this, her first written work, are abundantly in evidence, but in a slightly uproarious way. There are colourful images - "the sand dunes of my curves" ('I Fade From Pictures'); "clouds [...] an elevated sea in the mind of the atmosphere" ('You Never Cry Alone') - and strikingly expressed philosophical observations – "asking questions of our answers" ('The Answers'); "you have no choice in love, // your feelings are the spirit / of a cat, who imperiously does their own / thing, in their own time, without logic / or instruction." ('Love is the Spirit of a Cat', published in Acumen 101) - but some of the poems need bringing to heel, if I may put it that way. A demanding editor would perhaps strike out those rather distracting rhymes in otherwise free-verse poems and insist on lighter punctuation, but I have no wish to diminish Lopresti's achievement in bringing to us a most enjoyable baker's dozen of poems.

The poems in Katherine Lockton's debut pamphlet *Paper Doll* are altogether more sobering. They are outworkings of the quote at the head of her website: "Poetry is healing. When you write you go from being the victim to being the author." As a young child, Katherine fell from a very high window but survived by being caught in a blanket. She had to learn to walk again. There was physical healing but I sense that her poems are essential to the mental healing which is still going on. She has been a victim in other ways. She has written of how she was bullied as a child. Perhaps this is why she places so much emphasis as a teacher and facilitator on creating "a safe space", synonymous with that life-saving blanket, for her students to write in. This pamphlet finds her in her own safe space, creating a poetry of disarming frankness as she moves from victim to author.

The title *Paper Doll* is most apt. The poems exude fragility and femininity. Dolls appear in seven of the poems, and as paper dolls in three of the seven, most successfully in 'The Paper Doll Chain', a 'small but perfectly formed' poem and therefore difficult not to quote in full. Here is most of it: "One day I will become / this paper doll. I will have her skirt, thighs / and breasts that I will always think are too big. / I will try and cut her again and keep her safe / by making her smaller, and I will want to keep her / in a box. But she will defy me; time after time / teaching me how to live when she does."

Central to the pamphlet is the sequence 'After Rubix' in which the six colours of a Rubik's Cube are each considered in three parts: the colour itself, 'what [the colour] does', and 'what our parents don't say about [the colour]'. The sequence shows something of the surrealism which has so influenced the poetry of Latin America: "He puts himself into a bottle for her. At six-foot / - two his feet stick out. The way they always did / in bed. She uses his shoes to push him down."

Lockton is an Anglo-Bolivian 'Latinx' poet and writes as well in Spanish as she does in English. I enjoyed the two poems 'Mi Lengua' ('My Tongue') and 'Platanos Partidos' ('Split Bananas') in which Spanish lines are directly followed by lines of English translation as the poem progresses down the page – an interesting experiment; a clever representation of bi-lingualism.

The danger with a pamphlet that sets out to bring poetic healing from victimhood is that some of the poems may work against their creative purpose. 'The Angle' is so explicit in its description of child abuse that the reader may need mental healing after reading it. 'The Rape Scene' is so factual and protracted it reads disturbingly like diary notes of a rape and cuts itself off from poetry through its sheer horror. As a male, I cannot read such poems without a feeling of vicarious guilt and embarrassment, which is a shame. They detract from some very good work.

For spiritual healing, I turn to Neil Curry's *A Northumbrian Book of Hours*. The poet is returning to his beginnings. The first poem in his first collection *Ships in Bottles* (Enitharmon, 1988) was 'In a Calendar of Saints', a key component of many a Book of Hours, and referenced Cuthbert and Lindisfarne which stand at the centre of this sequence. Curry's second collection *Walking to Santiago* (Enitharmon, 1992) was a poetic pilgrimage along the Camino de Santiago to the tomb of St James in the Cathedral of Santiago de Compostela in north-west Spain. One of the most amusing poems in this poetic Book of Hours concerns the wanderings of Cuthbert's body as fleeing monks "trundled about with the coffin" through the north of England for seven years. Its eventual resting place was Durham Cathedral.

The pamphlet comprises a sequence of 14 short prose poems structured around the canonical 'Hours' of a medieval church day – Prime, Terce, Sext, Nones, Vespers, Compline – six poems of those names being interspersed with eight short narrative pieces. Owing much to Bede, the narrative poems relate the arrival at Lindisfarne of Aidan, its first bishop; his successor Cuthbert on the nearby island of Farne; Cuthbert's death and the subsequent desecration of Lindisfarne by the Vikings; and Cuthbert's posthumous adventures.

Curry's strengths are much in evidence – his quiet, conversational lines enriched with wry humour and a warmth which is respectful if not always reverent (the 'St' title is notably absent). I wondered as I opened this pamphlet how his understated style would rise to the meditative, numinous quality required for a Book of Hours; it doesn't, but then the sequence is clearly not intended to be religious beyond the history with which it deals. The poems do give a nod to the sacred writings in their use of language: "that trinity of killers, the bat, the badger and the screech-owl" ('Prime'); "on a hillside north of Melrose, a young Cuthbert, on watch over a sheepfold, beheld some great soul enter into heaven in a blaze of glory" ('5'); "Terrible were the portents – fiery dragons flying in the air" ('9'). But the wit triumphs: "Two heads may be better than one, but not, one would have thought, in a coffin. So, when Cuthbert's tomb was opened, King Oswald's was reverently removed, leaving the bishop – his body incorruptible and with the odour of sanctity still sweet about him – to have it all to himself again. Surely the very least any body could ask for." ('12')

So I don't find spiritual healing in *A Northumbrian Book of Hours*, but I do unhesitatingly recommend it. Curry has a special gift - amidst the everyday words, always perfectly chosen, he succeeds in introducing sudden moments of transcendence: "starfade" for dawn in 'Prime'; the description of puffins as "little brothers: a clown's face on a monk's robes" in 'Sext'; the otherwise ordinary but strangely sublime last line of 'Compline' (the evening prayer): "This day will not come again".

Speaking of wit, Hugo Williams is an acknowledged master. His anecdotal poems call to mind the writings of the much-missed Peter Ustinov. Just when we thought his fund of poems may have dried up, *Badlands* appears like a poetic "and there's more …"

But he is a seriously good poet. Behind and beyond the wit, he articulates with remarkable tenderness the seriousness and sadness of life. Take 'Silver Tears':

> Which I why I break open the lines,
> like breaking open a thermometer
> and seeing the little silver tears
> running around on the table-top.
> Line-breaks are time passing
> in slow motion, mimicking our fate
> with the terrible logic of gravity.
> They step down into the street
> or else they trip and fall
> through cracks in our expectations.

Brilliant. I won't quote any more, because I don't want to spoil any surprises. Read the pamphlet for yourself.

The last in our review of pamphlets is John Greening's *The Giddings*, an interweaving of verse and prose which continues his series of long 'dream poems'. Greening is a much-published, learned poet and critic, and I must trust to his forbearance as I respond to this latest work.

The poem is ambitious and difficult to get to grips with. But if you spend time with it, the poem repays the effort. The 'Argument' at its commencement, which puts the work into its historical context and explains the voices of the individual poems within, should be read and re-read before progressing. If I can summarise the 'Argument', a modern businessman at the end of a busy day, whether in a dream or actuality, follows a sign to the Giddings and walks off into the night. As he makes his way to Little Gidding he is addressed through poems by various trees – ash, elm, poplar, hawthorn, elder - and by a circle of trees as he arrives at Little Gidding church, where he encounters Nicholas Ferrar, founder of that village's seventeenth century spiritual community, in front of a huge fire on which are being burned Ferrar's collection of books. Whereupon Ferrar addresses him "in a formal canzone, the poem's centrepiece". A group of local "psalm-children" sing a poem to him. The trees then resume their poetry as time and the scenery move backwards through Ferrar's life – the London plague and his disastrous American business ventures which drove him from

London to this spiritual retreat, his European travels, and finally to his student days at Cambridge. Dawn breaks, all disappears, the businessman finds himself alone at Little Gidding, turns to lay "a birch twig with catkins, and a sprig of yew" on Ferrar's tomb, and returns to his Travelodge.

To set this poem as the dream or escapade of a modern businessman is stretching the bounds of a reader's credulity. Why then is the poet using this device? Because he is using the trees' and Ferrar's address to directly challenge our whole modern way of living:

> Those convoys sidling from their perimeter gate
> would hardly have noticed our ditch, or ever heard
> that such arcane and ancient forces might be wired
> (though souls at Gidding knew) into each dull black bud.
>
> (spoken by a huge ash tree, with reference to local convoys
> of cruise missiles wheeled out in the 1980s)

> How could one who never prays,
> whose life's a glistening web of all that's new,
> a distraction-maze, a constant reapprais-
> ing of romances, chances, fancies, praise—
> less sneer, cold compliment, and a brief her—
> oic moment, how could one such live praise—
> worthily with our group where how it prays
> is how it knows itself? And how, where hours
> are spent in cheerful prayer and psalm as ours
> have been, could one whose element is praise,
> whose aim is at the spirit first and last,
> how could that man survive, how even last

> A single hour in your future?   (from the central canzone)

Some awkward line-endings apart, the point is made.

The experimental approach, and a masterful versatility with form – from prose to free verse in the shape of trees to canzones to 16-syllable four-square stanzas – demonstrate an ambition to communicate spiritual meaning in a modern way whilst using the age-old voices of nature and history. The poet succeeds, almost.

ANDREW GEARY